IN PLACE
Jeremy Jones, Series Editor
Elena Passarello, Series Editor

Curing Season

LIBRARY OF
CONGRESS
SURPLUS
DUPLICATE

KRISTINE LANGLEY MAHLER

WEST VIRGINIA UNIVERSITY PRESS
MORGANTOWN

Copyright © 2022 by West Virginia University Press
All rights reserved
First edition published 2022 by West Virginia University Press
Printed in the United States of America

ISBN 978-1-952271-65-6 (paperback) / 978-1-952271-66-3 (ebook)

Library of Congress Cataloging-in-Publication Data
Names: Mahler, Kristine Langley, author.
Title: Curing season : artifacts / Kristine Langley Mahler.
Description: First edition. | Morgantown : West Virginia University Press,
    2022. | Series: In place | Includes bibliographical references.
Identifiers: LCCN 2022016286 | ISBN 9781952271656 (paperback) | ISBN
    9781952271663 (ebook)
Subjects: LCSH: Mahler, Kristine Langley—Childhood and youth. | Teenage
    girls—North Carolina—Biography. | Coming of age—North Carolina. |
    Belonging (Social psychology) | North Carolina—Biography. | BISAC:
    BIOGRAPHY & AUTOBIOGRAPHY / Personal Memoirs | BIOGRAPHY
    & AUTOBIOGRAPHY / Women
Classification: LCC F260.42.M34 A3 2022 | DDC 975.6/092 [B]—dc23/
    eng/20220427
LC record available at https://lccn.loc.gov/2022016286

Cover design by Amanda Weiss
Cover images courtesy of the author
Book design by Than Saffel / WVU Press

Essays in this collection have appeared, sometimes in different forms, in the
following publications: "Surface Tension," *Quarter After Eight* 24; "Club
Pines," *New Delta Review* 8, no. 1; "Shadowbox," *Pithead Chapel* 9, no. 12;
"Mädchenfänger," *DIAGRAM* 19, no. 6; "She'll Only Come Out at Night,"
CHEAP POP, February 2018; "Creepsake," *Hayden's Ferry Review*, Brief
Haunts, 2020; "Out Line," *Speculative Nonfiction* 4; "In the Burnpile Behind
the Old Nobles House," *Little Fiction/Big Truths*, Summer 2019; "Alignment,"
Blood Orange Review 12, no. 1; "Pull Me Through the Doorway" as "I Will Not
Die for You," *Rumpus*, Fall 2017, and as "Every Porch a Threshold," *Sundog
Lit* 16

for my girls

That there is pleasure in coming to grips with a body of knowledge, and that such pleasure is, in fact, inherent in the experience of learning itself, isn't anything most people in eastern North Carolina believe.

—Linda Flowers,
*Throwed Away: Failures of Progress
in Eastern North Carolina*

Contents

CURING SEASON

Surface Tension

Detachment

We had been released from one side of the country and dropped onto the other, landing in a doll house surrounded by pine trees taller than anything I'd seen before, nestled in a neighborhood so thickly forested I thought we'd moved into a campground. I was comforted because the pines reminded me of what we'd left behind. I expected to be absorbed. But where others might have put welcoming gardens, the houses in eastern North Carolina had undulating mounds of needles, and only azaleas thrived in their acidic soil—the stifled light, which barely filtered down, prevented anything else from growing. So I sat on the swing on our gracious front porch, beneath our slanted roofline, set back far enough from the road that I could barely be seen. In the middle of our suburban neighborhood, on the busiest street in the whole subdivision, I sat out there and no one saw me.

Flotation

There was a drainage ditch that snaked through the whole neighborhood, running behind the houses, connecting

Westhaven to Club Pines. Once, I released a pet crayfish into its shallow mud-choked waters, tired of the rancid marine smell in my bedroom. It had been a prize I'd won in school that I no longer needed because once I'd taken ownership and publicly named the crayfish after the girls whose favor I hoped to curry, we both lost our value. I dumped the crayfish and didn't even wait to see if Leila Annie Morgan tried to swim to its hopeless future or if it hovered on the surface, waiting to be taken back. If you want to live, you have to adapt.

I fantasized that during hurricane season, when it rained hard and the waters rose, I could take a raft down the ditch, paddling through the neighborhood. I would encroach on their property, belonging for that brief moment, and they'd never know.

Suspension

There were train tracks backboning it all, and I wonder what would have happened if I'd received the adolescence I claimed I'd wanted. I believed in the myth of teens making out in the abandoned, rusted car beside the tracks; believed in the fluids spilling all over the seats; believed the dirt-clod-clotted field must have seen kids running, hiding, dropping down out of sight, fumbling with clothes, rolling, the cigarettes. I believed in the old tobacco shack at the edge of the field that must have seen bottles and bottles of smuggled alcohol, the pop tabs that must be buried under all that dirt, and I wondered if, when the teenagers' teenagers were grown, the neighborhood would have to sprawl across the field to make way for new-comers; if, when they excavated the detritus, someone would try to piece a life together with the artifacts they'd found; or if, unlike me, they already knew what happened beneath the surface. I only knew I hadn't broken through.

Club Pines

My house

August on the coastal plains of North Carolina is like being shushed, like being smothered into agreement, a thick heat so relentless no one can raise a ruckus. Where I'd come from, August was packing season, August was leaving season, August was replacing season. But arriving in eastern North Carolina in August meant I had turned up outside the tobacco barns during curing season, the flue vents slightly propped open, hundred-year-old rafters the color of chaw juice hung with sheaves, the stifling, unbearable heat a recognized seasoning that the native plant welcomed—it was the only way to transform into what people wanted.

August in eastern North Carolina looks like industry and productivity, but it lapses back into indolence because curing season only lasts one week. The grass is yellow and the air is yellow and so are the dried-out needles from the skinny pine trees soaring eighty feet in the air, lining the streets of my new neighborhood and looking like a permutation of my old home on the conifered slopes of Oregon's Willamette Valley.

We hadn't had enough money to live up in the tree-filled hills—we'd lived down in the flats—but enough Californians had carpetbagged north that by the time my parents sold their little 1950s ranch, the house had doubled in value, netting enough to buy us into Club Pines, this upper-middle-class suburban neighborhood on the southwest side of town, away from both "the urban element" and the university where my father would work.

My new house was nooked into a corner pocket off Club Pines' main boulevard, the center of the center, a road everyone had to travel. That comforted me, because while the pine trees felt like home, they only formed a facsimile of forest; they stood in clusters like gossipy girls outside the cafeteria, denuded trunks only branching out in the top quarters, boughs whispering a language to each other that you had to have been there long enough to understand. Slurred, drawled, words confused, fuzzy meanings, phrases I'd never heard before, a code I wanted to crack.

The pine trees obscured my house from the road. The storms hadn't come yet.

Carleigh's house
Something has been stolen and it needs to be recovered. On the day we'd moved into our new house, Carleigh crossed the cul-de-sac to scout the scene. I unpacked my Monopoly board, trying to show her that playing House Rules with a bonus $500 every time we passed GO made the game more fun—the way my neighbor and I used to play—but Carleigh was disinterested. She had watched as I arranged my special

belongings onto my dresser: an old puzzle piece of Indiana, a rock from a place I couldn't even remember, a bookmark with a cheetah on it, a half-dollar my grandma had given me, the pin I'd made in Campfire Girls with melted plastic. A day or two after Carleigh left, I am still trying to surround myself with the physical reminders that I have a past when I notice my pin is missing. This house is too clean, too un-lived-in. I know where it has gone. So I knock on Carleigh's door, ask her if she wants to play. She lets me in, and in her downstairs TV room we watch a half hour of *Eureeka's Castle* before I excuse myself to the bathroom. But I don't go to the downstairs half bath. I go upstairs to her bedroom. It's easy enough to find; it's obvious enough. And Carleigh doesn't even to know how to hide it: my pin is sitting right on top of her dresser. I scoop my pin into my pocket and quickly leave her bedroom as Carleigh bounds upstairs, suspiciously pointing out the bathroom down the hall, and I pretend I was lost, and Carleigh goes into her room and I can see her look on her dresser before I close the bathroom door but when I come back out, claiming my mom is probably looking for me and I should go home, Carleigh doesn't have the nerve to accuse me of stealing. Stealing what. Stealing back.

Michelle's house

Somehow I broker an invitation to Michelle's house even though she is best friends with Carleigh. On request, I bring my troll dolls and Michelle and I play a game where we hide them in her front parlor, and even though I know I'd brought seven trolls, we can only find six: the blue-haired one, the one in a kimono, the overalls one, the other one, the other one, the other one. I can't remember which troll is missing from my collection, which is my fault. Michelle does not invite me over again when she discovers I am, like most of our neighborhood, being bused from our suburb to desegregate the urban public schools. She is a St. Peter's girl. I sneer because I may be a pleb, but she is a snob.

Taylor's house
An upstairs bonus room, Tom Cruise in *Cocktail* on her private VCR; we will get in trouble for watching an R-rated movie, but how can you expect us to be surrounded by adult movies and choose *Aladdin*? We unroll our sleeping bags onto the sectional, and then we brush our teeth downstairs in the bathroom that Taylor has to clean every day. There is a special spray cleaner she has to use in the shower, and a special sponge, and until I had to wait for her to finish her after-school chores, I hadn't realized people ever cleaned their showers. All that soap splashing off our bodies doesn't clean the tile walls? Taylor's house backs up to a wooded ditch with an abandoned half fort near a swampy pond, and there's a barbed-wire fence it's easy to bend our bodies between; we don't get caught on it, even in the dark, and we walk into the tobacco fields behind our neighborhood, hurling dirt clods as far as we can, watching them explode into puffs of smoke in the humid moonlight.

Georgia's house
Thick cigarette smoke, stale cigarette smoke, cigarette smoke

hanging in the kitchen like oxygen, cigarette smoke like we're exactly where we are, in the heart of tobacco country, where it's patriotic to smoke, where it's a legacy to smoke, where discarded soft-packs line the gutters. Georgia claims her parents only smoke outside, but the house smells like an ashtray. I've never been in a house where the parents smoke. Where her teenage sister smokes. Where everything is so saturated with smoke I worry that I'm going to get lung cancer just by staying overnight. I can't fall asleep at Georgia's house. I watch *SNL* until midnight because no one has a bedtime. No rules. I ride my bike home at first light and my mom throws my sleeping bag and Nanny, my baby blanket, directly into the washing machine.

Katy's house

Her mom has macaroni and cheese waiting when Katy gets home from school and Katy eats dinner at 4 p.m., sitting at the round kitchen table alone, and I've never heard of eating so early and I've also never eaten dinner without my parents and siblings. Afterwards, I introduce Dirty Barbies to Katy even though we are ten and I assume she's played this game before. She has, and she knows new narratives. Her older brother sleeps in a huge addition at the back, a bonus room nearly as large as the rest of the house. Katy explains that the boys get all the good stuff. We watch syndicated *Saved by the Bell* episodes and Katy loves blond Zack Morris, who looks like my crush from my old life. Katy tells me that boys like big butts and she sticks out her behind and wiggles it proudly, and I've never considered my butt as a reason a boy might like me but if Katy says it and Sir Mix-a-Lot says it, I guess it's true. I don't know how to counteract the fear that mine is so flat it fades into obscurity.

Kim's house

Sweet baby Kim, a little blond sprite of a child, tiny with glasses, and we are the same age but I can't stop thinking of her as my younger sister. Kim is an only child. Kim has a bedroom with a white frilly canopy bed and Kim has an upstairs playroom larger than my living room, all to herself. Every toy I ever wanted. Every toy I ever saw advertised on TV. A dollhouse and a Lite Brite and puzzles and Cabbage Patch Kids and Kim has the baby doll that poops in a diaper and I get to help her change the diaper when the poop comes out orange and it all feels so helpless, watching Kim with her little fake baby's diaper. I want to be enchanted by the infinitesimally tiny teacups and saucers carefully placed on the dollhouse dining table; I want to agree to nestling our bodies in the double beanbag by the overflowing bookcase, engrossed in reading aloud from the old red book of Disney stories, but I also want to be with Georgia and Katy, skidding our bikes around the neighborhood, trumpeting, "That's fucking shit!" just because we can, just because we know we are growing up.

Leila's house

Smells like Glade Plug-Ins and some foreign spice whose origin I never find out. Leila lives in a large, brick two-story-with-third-floor-dormers, white muntined windows, black show-shutters, white pillars holding up a porticoed entry roof, a house presenting its success at blending into the neighborhood. We make paper fortune-tellers on the back screen porch, and we both choose Ryan's name to be matched with Silver because we both love him and we both love silver. Leila's brother Farooq has the larger bedroom because he is a boy. In Leila's bedroom, I think there are two twin beds, but I don't make it that long; I don't even make it to bedtime before I panic—I'm too far from home—and I make the call, bewildering Leila's mom, who continues to ask what she can do to make me more comfortable until my mom arrives.

Annie's house

I almost know it better than my own after spending countless nights twinned with my best friend, while she was still my best friend. With my eyes closed, I can map out the main level with the sunroom and the oversized formal living room, the four bedrooms and bathrooms and the bonus room on the second story; I know the size of her parents' bathroom and which two bedrooms Annie owned and I slept in—the small one at the top of the stairs when her sister still lived at home, and the bedroom nooked in the corner behind the stairwell where Annie, later, hooked up her grow lights. We tried to watch a murder mystery ghost video in the sunroom, we slapped together vanilla cupcakes with Egg Beaters in the kitchen, we never went in the formal dining room. No one went in the formal dining room. I know the shallow backyard where our collies cautiously sniffed each other, I know the three-car garage where her hamster cage was kept, I know the corner of the counter with the cordless phone dock, where

Annie would call to ask if I wanted to come over and play, when we still called it "playing," when I still anticipated her calls, when she was still my best friend, when she was still.

Elise's house
A word-association poem tucked under magnets on her parents' fridge that I copy, almost word for word, replacing lines like "Mary Tyler Moore . . . apples" with "Hillary Rodham Clinton . . . oranges," so derivative it embarrassed me later. A "company" where we personalize notebooks with our paint pens purchased at Bender-Burkot for $5.95 each; I was assigned to buy Carolina blue and silver, and I was expected to donate them to the company for usage, but it was a rip-off because Elise took all the "business" for herself. Elise has moles in strangely symmetrical curves on her hands, like parentheses. Elise is tall. Elise's mom is an occupational therapist named Denise and her father's job doesn't matter but his name is Stan, and Elise calls her parents Stan and Denise and she is their only child. They have a huge compost heap in the back of their yard covered with pine needles. When Elise comes to my house for my eleventh birthday party, she drinks three large glasses of milk in quick succession. Elise has a mystery club and a notebook like Harriet the Spy and she is constantly surveilling and she invents a symbol to sign her notes, which is a clear sign she has been watching Annie and me. Elise starts another club called GGC and it means Gorgeous Guys Club and it is no secret that the only point of this club is to talk about the boys she thinks are gorgeous and I am supposed to agree.

Joanne's house

Bologna. The house smells like bologna. I spend a lot of time at Joanne's house because she lives right down the road and her mom works late and she doesn't have a father anymore. Her older brother watches MTV, and we're not allowed to watch MTV at my house, so I'm at Joanne's house when I see Pearl Jam's video for "Jeremy." I'd never realized someone could bring a gun to school. Joanne's bedroom is huge and has a dormer window, while her brother is snuffed into a little bedroom to the right of the staircase. Eventually Joanne will have to share her bedroom with her new stepsister on weekends, and I will stop coming over to play with Joanne because I prefer hanging out with her sarcastic stepsister, but right now Joanne shows me her American Girl doll and her brass doll bed, and we play computer games side by side on separate computers in the computer room. I play King's Quest V and Joanne plays Lemmings. We rarely speak.

Heather's house

A white cockatoo screaming from its cage in the corner, a baby brother rug-burning his knees, parents sitting under their Christmas-lights-strung gazebo in the backyard drinking cocktails and listening to Jimmy Buffett. A twin bed, a sleeping bag on the floor beside it, a poster of Vanilla Ice that Heather confesses she kisses regularly. A small bedroom. A room stuffed with the sort of ephemera you collect on vacation, backscratchers and pillows and seashell collections. Heather curses but she isn't like Georgia or Katy; Heather doesn't know when it's appropriate, Heather doesn't know

you're supposed to hide it from my parents. I leave before
9 p.m., claiming a stomachache, Heather's mom blowzily
proclaiming her sympathy after being summoned from the
gazebo, Heather whining that they've got Pepto-Bismol. I
rush out of the house when I see the headlights of our minivan; my mom doesn't even make it to the front door.

Sangeeta's house
One story, which is unusual in our neighborhood. Brick.
Windows with the plantation blinds always pulled. New-ish,
but nothing to remark on. Three cars in the driveway, which
makes no sense since I think Sangeeta is the oldest and she's
only twelve. Who needs three cars with two adults? Maybe
there are not two adults. Maybe Sangeeta's grandma lives
with them. But no one's grandma lives with them; everyone's
grandma lives *near* them. Maybe someone on the bus asked her
about it once, but Sangeeta probably volunteered the information and anyway, it doesn't really matter. Sangeeta's house
is in the right location, but no one is paying attention. For
Christmas, Sangeeta buys sets of fake pearl-drop necklaces,
bracelets, and anklets from Claire's and distributes them to me
and the other girls who've allowed her to sit at our lunch table.
No one wears pearls—that will come when the other girls are
debutantes, but by then, no one will accept imitations.

Gretchen's house
After Annie, I sleep here. I sleep in Gretchen's bedroom at the
front of the house and Gretchen falls asleep listening to the
Beatles and since I can't sleep through background noise, I

wait until the CD has finished before sliding out of my sleeping bag and quietly, guiltily, stopping it from starting again. I sit on the carpet of Gretchen's bedroom and I write stupid slurs about Annie in Gretchen's yearbook and I am in Gretchen's bedroom weeks later when I flip to my page and find a whole diatribe of cruelty Annie has scrawled all over my face. Gretchen is neutral ground, Gretchen is friends with us both, but Gretchen's house is so close to Annie's that I know there must be warm summer nights when they meet up on the street without me and I will not know what they say. Not until Annie wants me to know what they say.

Aimee's house
Taylor tells me she's going to be friends with Aimee again since summer is coming up and Aimee has a pool, so I decide to try to be friends with Aimee too. Aimee's house is also on a corner lot like mine, but while my house is veiled behind the pine trees, hers sits proud, front and center, no need to hide. I bring my Get Along Gang towel to Aimee's house because it is cool and vintage, and in seventh grade, it's funny to act like we're still into our childhoods. The towel is thin, and when I wrap it around my body, I soak through the towel immediately. I'm still wearing a corny old one-piece with bright neon pink and orange straps. I don't know where Aimee and Taylor have gotten their swimsuits, but it was somewhere geared for teens, maybe the juniors' section at Brody's, but definitely not the kids' rack at Walmart. I leave my towel behind "on accident" since Aimee didn't comment on it; she'll have to return my towel to me at some point and surely she'll have a quip

about it and that will make us friends. But the towel seems to vanish, or her attention vanishes, because two weeks later I haven't gotten a phone call from Aimee so I call her and ask if I left a towel behind, *Get Along Gang on it haha remember them*? She drawls no.

Later, Gretchen gets me invited to a sleepover in Aimee's third-floor attic, and Aimee gets inexplicably sad listening to "I'll Never Get Over You (Getting Over Me)" and we are all mystified since Aimee isn't dating anyone at school and never has, so we assume it was some boy she met at her beach house on the Outer Banks. Aimee refuses to speak about it, and in the morning, Aimee has left us all upstairs, and she's sleeping in her bed on the second floor, and I awkwardly slip out without saying goodbye, walking the neighborhood streets back to my house.

Rie's house
A two-story vaulted ceiling in the living room, a piano in the living room where Rie's mom makes her practice immediately after school, where Rie is practicing when Gretchen and I come over. I don't remember why we come over. Rie is not allowed to leave with us. Rie tries to teach us how to pronounce her name; I say "Ree-ay" and she shakes her head. Gretchen says "Ree" and she shakes her head. "Rlee-ay," she says. We repeat, "Lee-ay" and she shakes her head. "Rlee-ay." We cannot get it right.

Laura's house
We aren't friends; we're just on the school softball team

together. Everyone knows Laura and Elise are best friends, but Elise must be out of town because Laura's dad comes and picks me up, dropping me and Laura off at the town festival. Laura's dad gives us twenty bucks and Laura and I fill vases with colored sand and we eat an elephant ear and walk around the three-block-long scene, stopping underneath the awnings of the tents, trying to get some shade in the humid summer. I go back to Laura's house when we're done being hot, and we sit in her bedroom with a window that faces the street, a bedroom positioned at the very front of the house, and while Laura's an only child just like Elise, just like Kim, I don't feel her privilege. I stare out her front window at Annie's old house, wondering what Laura has also seen.

Catherine's house

Catherine's younger sister was more intuitive. Catherine's younger sister would turn around and perch her elbows on the back of the seat to talk to me on our way to a softball game in Ayden-Grifton. I was sitting on a bus bench by myself, ostensibly because we had the space and it felt invasively close to sit beside another girl when there were clearly enough seats for us to spread out, but really because everyone knew my only friend now was Gretchen, and she didn't play softball. Catherine was on the softball team too but her little sister was the one who'd talk to me. Catherine had other fish to fry, other girls whose friendship she'd sought, other girls who were popular and had something to offer. I go to Catherine's house once, when Gretchen cajoles me to come over, calling from Catherine's phone, and it feels like a strange ruse because Gretchen leaves Catherine's three minutes after I arrive, and I sit in Catherine's bedroom for twenty minutes and for what? Because it is a ruse. Because Gretchen planned a surprise birthday/going away party for me, and she has biked to my house and is helping my parents tie balloons to the deck posts.

Catherine shuffles me out of her house by pretending she just remembered she was going to meet someone at the park, and I know how to read the signs that I'm not wanted anymore. I return home and am met at the front door by my mom, who walks me to the backyard with my eyes blindfolded, and the CD player is queued up to begin blaring John and Paul as they yell, possessively, that if I'd thought it was *my* birthday, they're gonna correct me—it's *their* birthday too, yeah, and when the blindfold is removed, standing in a half circle on my deck, sweating in a puncture-hole of thick sunlight—once blocked by the pine tree which had storm-crashed into our house—there are four girls whose houses I've never been inside, who don't even live in my neighborhood, and Gretchen is there front and center and I know the only reason the others have come is because Gretchen asked them; I am certain no one is going to miss me when I'm gone.

Shadowbox

It was a hollowed wooden square, a frame with frames within it, empty boxes waiting to be filled with belongings. It was built out of golden oak slivers my father had painstakingly cut and glued into a miniature cabinet of curiosities, one of the most delicate gifts he had ever assembled, meant to match the southern country-style house to which we'd moved. My mother called it a shadow box, but I always thought it was shadowbox, eliding the two words together and taking on an alternate meaning: to shadowbox is to swing at an imaginary foe.

Naval lore warns that a sailor's shadow shouldn't touch his home shore before his physical body can, and risking the unlucky split of a sunray through a scrim of fog is too unpredictable, uncontrollable. So a returning sailor crates up his personal effects as a "shadow" of himself, bearing the box in his arms, corporeal feet sinking into sand a second before his talismanic self comes ashore. It is a superstition with a haunting premise: your belongings can absorb you. Your possessions can swallow up the gray and ghostly leavings of your other self, alchemizing mundane objects into fetishes meaningless to anyone but you. And I had left my self behind, though I'd carried all of my possessions with me across the country, touching my ten-year-old toe onto the hard-packed pine needles of North Carolina.

My father, a sailor's son, constructed tables and cabinets and frames he saw in *Fine Woodworking* magazines. I was proud of the furniture my father had built for our family, and I would tour new friends through my house, announcing, "Basically, if you see something wooden, my dad made it." They seemed impressed with the first few items, but their faces would begin to wilt as I led them to marvel at another frame, another side table. I would pick up on the girls' waning interest, but I was still convinced that it would be the *next* piece—the TV cabinet! or the quilt rack!—which would grant me some sort of by-producted appeal. I was a sidewinder trying to coil into friendships that weren't much more than a gesture, a lunch conversation one Tuesday, a week-long science project that required a partner. Each interaction was an emblem of an outstretched hand, I thought, but when I would place them together to compile a collection of interest, they didn't add up; each hand reaching out was mine.

A shadowbox is meant to hold representations of the life its owner has lived, the mementoes of moments that need physical representation, manifestation, the emblems of success. But a shadowbox is also a military

tradition, a glass-walled trapping of evidence that bat-
tles had been fought, helmets stolen off the field, insig-
nia and rank indicating the highest rung climbed. When
my father built our shadowbox, I had just ducked into
the foxhole of middle school.

A piece of computer paper scissored into a triangle, crumpled and unfolded and recrumpled, a quarter-teaspoon of oregano sprinkled in the center and rolled up like a burrito, the loose flap secured with a dot of Elmer's. The girl was so stupid she wouldn't know the difference, my friend said, because she would be so eager to partake. I laughed along with my friend as she braided my hair and we watched MTV and we never delivered the fake joint, but whenever my mom served spaghetti, I leaned eagerly toward the plate, hoping to catch a whiff of the forbidden, not knowing the difference.

Squirreled in the bottom of a wallpaper-fabric box on the top shelf of an ignored closet, the breakup letter I wrote to my friend two years earlier.

Another girl had goaded me, and I wanted to be more meaningful to that girl, so I delivered the letter while she waited at the end of the street. Within minutes of arriving home, I hopped back on my bike and pedaled and snatched that smash letter off my friend's doorstep before she ever saw it.

It flushed my cheeks with shame in the years to come when I remembered the letter existed, but I didn't get rid of it. It was a treachery I needed to remember I had not committed.

Initials were stitched into the

monogrammed back-packs of the girls who had received their mothers' names as their own first names.

I created a symbol featuring those middle initials, unified and linking off one another, to demonstrate my loyalty to girls who never asked me to belong, only adding my K as a small afterthought, a hanger-on-the-bottom.

Jessie Jenna Blaire Beth Morgan Pamela Lesley Lindsay Kristin Kristen Kristine.

Navy blue wide-wale corduroy pant legs lopped off, loose like sleeves. A six-inch gray halo trimmed off a $6 baby doll tee from Walmart. The castoffs of my debut outfit my friend had helped me assemble; I was going to appear in the doorway of

A peace-frog patch, green legs splayed out with nothing to hide. I bought it at a mall in Richmond, Virginia, on our chaperoned school band trip, the hotel hot tub stuffed with eighth graders, my clarinet case lonely on the floor of the hotel room where the VFW hall where two cool girls were sharing a birthday party and stun everyone with my transformation into Hot Grunge Girl with my bare midriff and the thrifted cords my friend had sewn into a short skirt. But the day of the party was too cold. I wore my dad's V-neck sweater and baggy jeans, desexed grunge that let me hide what had not changed, lurking behind my friend as we arrived and she was greeted.

My friend's radio-dubbed cassette tape of All-4-One's "I Swear," a song I mocked for its sentimentality, preferring decisiveness over promises and pleas.

But my friend loved the song, so we rewound and played and rewound and played it that weekend at her beach house,

we "got lucky" with only three girls assigned. I had one of the two double beds to myself. I could hear the other girls' soft murmurs negotiating space as they turned over, tentatively touching ankles, and I tucked my legs up tight, curled in, to make room for no one.

walking the shoreline
watching for cute
boys, slipping into
our swimsuits and
showering together
to try out all of the
shampoos, lying in
our side-by-side twin
beds, afraid of the
roaches in the room
corners, and petu-
lantly refusing to be
the one to get up and
turn out the lights,
stubborn and scared,
and even now, as the
melisma is dying out
at the end of "I-I-
I-I-I swe-e-e-ear,"
I can still hear the
DJ overlaying "96.3
The Hot—" a sharp
cut truncating what
was left unspoken.

Historically, curiosity cabinets were assembled to show off, to establish societal rank, to impress. Sir Ashton Lever, an eighteenth-century English gentryman, began collecting seashells when he was thirty-one years old, a youthful whimsy which seems to hint at an arrested development. Lever's collection snowballed into fossils and feathers and bones and teeth and antlers and joints, and the year before America browbeat Britain into accepting its independence, Lever rented a large estate in London to display his "natural ephemera." Lever's display of his acquisitions was a success for ten years, but public interest was bound to fade.

Lever tried to sell his tired collection to the British Museum, but if not the museum, maybe Catherine II of Russia would be interested? Both declined, disinterested in Lever's grasping attempt to profit off an ungainly collection that had ultimately featured anything Lever thought might have attracted anyone ever. In a final blaze of glory, Lever offered his entire collection up in a lottery. He only sold eight thousand tickets; he had hoped to sell thirty-six thousand. Two years later, Lever committed suicide.

Cabinets of curiosities are filled with artifacts that weren't created by the collector—they have been, instead, smuggled away from their resting places and are presented to the public out of context. When viewed on display, the artifacts are supposed to reflect on the collector's sensibilities, like the very nature of assimilating the items can be transmuted as her foresight into their worth. When, at fourteen, I took new midwestern friends by the elbow, guiding them through the Carolina Kristine Museum, what I wanted them to notice most was my Very Brave Recognition that my preserved hurts were totems of the times I had tried and failed. They were bomb shrapnel I kept as a warning to myself.

A vertebra, a coin, a basket, a skull. A death mask, a sandstone tablet, a stuffed extinct bird. A patch, a joint, a letter never sent, the cast-off leavings of a look in a wooden frame my father built, holding the shadows of the self I bore in my arms every time I stepped onto an unfamiliar shore.

A Fixed Plot

To write about the graveyard at the mall is to avoid the metaphor of the mall as graveyard, which has become a trope without teeth. Everyone already knows traditional malls are dead. Malls are haunted by the ghosts of the adolescents we once were, Teen Spirit stench cobwebbed in the high ceiling corners, empty benches bowed by that old desperation to belong—that feeling I came to the mall to obscure.

I was raised as a suburban girl and so malls have always been places of transformation, a collection of commerce promising that a fistful of bills could turn my white Keds-knockoffs into two-toned Simples, alchemizing me from unpopular to popular. If money was spent in the right stores on the right items with the right labels, if I was carrying the right shopping bag through the right food court when the right kids were waiting to be picked up by their parents, I was sure I could purchase my way into position.

§

In 1663, the King of England granted proprietary rights over North Carolina land to eight men, the Lords Proprietors. Seven of the proprietors sold their shares, by royal request, back to the Crown in 1729, but not Sir John Carteret, great-grandson and inheritor to the estate of the single remaining Lord Proprietor, the Earl of Granville. The Crown frowned at the disobedience of Sir John, who finally agreed to surrender any claim on the rest of North Carolina in exchange for the ability to hold tight to the land that was his—a sixty-mile-long strip along the top of the state, scooping up what would become Greenville and Pitt County.

§

When I was ten, my family moved to Greenville, a town on eastern North Carolina's coastal plains that was surrounded by three-hundred-year-old tobacco fields. I was an archaeology-obsessed child, collecting information from the artifacts of Pitt County they'd proudly put on display in the white-columned town library. I was enthralled by the history of my new homeland. I didn't know that it hadn't actually become my new homeland. That my sheer presence in a place didn't convey belonging. It didn't take long to learn.

There were two malls in Greenville. The Carolina East Mall was located across the highway from the neighborhood into which I'd moved. I would ride my bike to the Carolina East, a dollar and a nickel tucked into my front jeans pocket, and wait in line at K&M Cafeteria behind the old folks for a slice of cheesecake. I accompanied my mom as she purchased miniature brass teapots and tiny wooden flour and sugar canisters from Millie's for her shadow box. The Carolina East was dying, even in the midnineties; it was easy to steal a rainbow star pin from the dollar store to smack on my backpack like the cool girls in my grade.

But the Real Mall was near the university, and it was called The Plaza. The Plaza had better stores—the big Brody's with the huge juniors' section, the larger Belk, the Glamour Shots, the Afterthoughts, the Bath & Body Works purveying the spray lotions that were required in the Eppes Middle School girls' locker room, the Take Ten where I swapped quarters for tokens, directing the claw over and over again, the prize always slipping out of my grip.

Versions of ourselves died every time we entered a mall; at least I wished they did.

§

In the parking lot of The Plaza, there is a walled-in cemetery. A four-foot-high brick fence surrounds a graveyard with tombstones jutting through the cement. I couldn't believe it when I'd first peered over the wall, walking from my mom's parking spot to the mall entrance—a cemetery? At the mall? The NICE mall? White weathered marble is spaced in even rows, with a few newer-looking granite stones—the names on those markers are easier to read.

The cemetery is filled with the Evanses' dead: the Evanses of the eponymous street bisecting Greenville, the Evanses tracing back to Richard Evans, town founder, who had staked his claim nearly three hundred years earlier, securing his family in place. There was an Evans girl in my grade, though I never went to X's house, never called her—we weren't even in classes together—we just played on the same school basketball team one year, softball another. She wore tomboyish long shorts, even though fingertip-length was in fashion; oversized T-shirts; pulling her hair into a low-slung ponytail every day like a burden she didn't want to acknowledge but could not remove.

§

I have spent a lot of time looking up the Evanses. I suppose I'm looking for those missing teeth from the sharks, sown in the million-year-old mud of Greens Mill Run—the creek entrenched in the land the Evanses once owned. Own. I know how to access the Pitt County property records website. I looked for the evidence of longevity, the griphooks in the ground, because I wanted to white-knuckle their comfort, squeezing until it turned into a curse.

When I lived in Greenville, history was embedded in nomenclature. Girls had the same names as their mothers, boys were either III and IV, or their first names were their mothers' maiden names. The counties continued to generate their ancient namesakes; there was a Rowan and a Cartrette—the outgrowth of Sir John Carteret—in my grade. My new teacher asked me what school I'd moved from, and I answered "Wilson." My teacher smiled and named a couple of teachers she knew "up in Wilson," and I realized she thought I had moved from Wilson, North Carolina—a town forty miles away from Greenville. I corrected my teacher, disclosing that my school was actually named Wilson Elementary—I had moved from Oregon—and she grew disinterested, snapping "Oh," before turning away and beginning class, "Anyway."

I recite the story of cotillion again, that narrative of exclusion that never wavers no matter how often I tell it—how the Pitt County parents of fifth graders in Lynndale and Brook Valley and Lake Ellsworth and my neighborhood received registration materials, and my bewildered Minnesota-raised parents asked me once, in passing, if I was interested. Of course I refused. I was ten and terrified of boys. I didn't know that I was the only girl from Club Pines who would not attend. I cannot be certain I was the only girl from Club Pines who did not attend. But in the bleachers before school on the mornings after cotillion classes, I felt like the only girl who'd not seen a sweaty palm reaching out as "Build Me Up Buttercup" began Carolina-shagging, the only girl not retracing the old swing-steps of her parents' summer romances out on Emerald Isle.

I have a memory of my school bus driver picking up the Evans girl in the morning, once, from a house I admired on a lot that bordered Greens Mill Run—the big white-pillared house that looks exactly like Tara in *Gone with the Wind*. But after researching the property, I can't connect the longtime owners of the home with the Evanses, or with X's mother's family. Maybe I have just sited X there, standing with purpose in a place that looked most like what I'd imagined belonging to the South would.

§

John Evans, a second-generation Virginian, bought two hundred acres of Pitt County land in 1747.

↓

Moses Evans, son of John, was one of the first owners of lots in Greenville and bought his land from a "relative," Richard Evans—the founder of Greenville.

↓

John S. Evans, son of Moses, owned the land on which Pitt Plaza (later, The Plaza) was built.

↓

Amos Evans was one of the sons of John S. Evans. Amos's brothers Abner, John, and William Franklin's families are the ones buried at the mall. Amos's brother James Lewis sold their father's land to the company who constructed Pitt Plaza.

↓

Godfrey Evans, son of Amos.

↓

Leslie Evans, son of Godfrey.

↓

James Evans, son of Leslie.

↓

X, daughter of James.

§

It alarms me how adept I am at tracing the lineage of a girl I barely knew. I suppose I could contact X—I know how, I've seen her Facebook profile, I know she's a receptionist at a dental clinic (*such ignominy*, I think, *for an Evans!*). She probably doesn't even remember my name. I could put up a good explanatory front—"I'm a writer, doing research on the early founders of Pitt County, and I traced your $5^\times$-great-grandfather's line and it led to you"—and I don't have to look creepy. I'm just a journalist with a few fill-in-these-blanks questions. But I love the archival research, the feeling of discovery, the uncovering, the revelations that I can piece together by finding all the right elements. The information has always been right there, unobstructed, but it's obvious only to those who know how to look. Every time I compress reported facts into truth, I am proving that I am worthy.

Evans Street is the westernmost border for Lynndale, a neighborhood with county heritage street names like Granville and Martinsborough. Evans Street cleaves Greenville, running south all the way from the town commons on the Tar River. The county courthouse is on Evans Street. The city library is on Evans Street. The Greenville Museum of Art is on Evans Street. Evans Street was also the home of the old Eveready plant, a dead gray monolith that kids used to whisper was haunted. Someone knocked the factory down sometime after 1996; a strip mall has been built atop its Superfund remains.

The Eveready plant used to dump its waste in a landfill a few hundred feet north of St. Peter's, the Catholic church I attended in Greenville. The Eveready landfill is just north of the cemetery where anonymous Catholics—the closest claim I had to "my" people in Greenville—were buried. The landfill is also three blocks north of the park where I used to tentatively wade in Greens Mill Run, after church, to collect shark teeth.

§

It's kitsch, the shock and headshake of posting photographs online of a cemetery outside a mall. Desecration, degradation, the past butted up against the economic present. Daddy won't sell the farm until he does, save the family cemetery and a twelve-foot right-of-way to Greenville Boulevard for a private lane so the Evanses can process unencumbered each Decoration Day.

It's not even called The Plaza anymore. Some years after I moved away, the mall received a rebrand, the new owners retitling it Colonial Mall. After the eventual death of the Carolina East Mall, the last man standing in town—The old Plaza—dropped the colonist connotations to assert its boring, simple, monolithic current name: Greenville Mall.

§

There's a blog post touting the Evans cemetery at The Plaza— in fact, the Evans cemetery inspired a "new feature" on a website called Cemetery Space. An anonymous commenter, in 2010, mentioned: "I've always walked passed [*sic*] and looked at this cemetery when I went to the mall since I was little and never knew until a few years ago that I was related to them. My grandmother Sallie Buck (Evans) is 103, and this is her family."

A few clicks here, a few clicks there, I can connect who the likely commenter was by following the Evans family tree.

Cemetery Space was abandoned sometime after 2015. Cemetery Space's webmaster was obviously a Pitt County Greenvillian—the first "Video Visit" feature was to the Black section of a Greenville cemetery, and the second one highlighted a small cemetery located by the Hardee Chapel in—you guessed it—Greenville.

Eastern North Carolina is well known for the prevalence of graves located on private family land rather than graves neatly boxed into churchyards. In a 2007 *New York Times* article, a Pitt County resident describes how his family's graves—including that of his great-uncle, a Civil War veteran—were recently moved for commercial development. A few years prior to the interview, the Pitt County man had also been contacted when a subdivision was built next to his grandfather's grave, and the developers decided to fence off the cemetery containing the grave rather than unearth it.

A man visiting eastern North Carolina in 2010 asked, in a City-Data forum, why he saw so many graves in peoples' front yards. A knowledgeable North Carolinian assured the confused Yankee, "There are strict laws about desecrating graves here. You can't just bulldoze them for developments. They have to be reintered [*sic*], like the graves at the Pitt County Courthouse, or not disturbed at all." A commenter identifying themself as located in Pitt County chimed in, "I have seen at least 5 homes . . . that had graves on the property that seemed to be at least 100 years old so I'm surprised that more real estate agents weren't aware [of the situation]."

The wise forum respondent retorted, "I doubt the real estate agents didn't truly know the reason [for the gravestones], unless they were transplants themselves."

Dead on the front lawns, dead in the front parking lots. Bodies in coffins are supposed to soften into soil, though at The Plaza, there will be no digging up, no reburial. April M left a comment on a 2012 blog post by a "midwestern mom gone southern" who had photographed the Evans cemetery, asserting that "there is an old law in north carolina that says if a family does not give permission a family cemetery can't be moves [*sic*]. So if all the members are dead you have no one to ask."

But April M was wrong. I scoured the North Carolina state laws until I found the official state code, which states explicitly that the only permission needed comes from the governing body of the municipality or county in which a cemetery is located. Thirty days' notice must be made to the next of kin before digging, but the dead can be moved, no question.

And trust me: the Evanses are still in town. I am the one who is not. I slipped out of Greenville between middle and high school, a class photo in a 1996 Eppes yearbook titled "THESE ARE THE DAYS" my only lasting legacy.

§

The dead buried in the Evans family cemetery at The Plaza are all X's great-great-grandfather Amos's brothers and sisters and their families. Amos's family is buried out by the Rose

High School football stadium. I follow the Cemetery Census directions to the family cemetery of Amos Evans, scrolling in on Google Maps. The cemetery is barely obscured by what must be a mini hedgerow—X's great-great-grandfather is interred less than twenty feet from the track, maybe fifty feet from the stadium seating at Rose, where I once sat and cheered for the Eppes football team. This stamp of a burial plot was ghosting over X—I know she went to Rose. Don't ask me how I know. It doesn't take much sleuthing. Her great-grandfather Godfrey is not buried out there, however, so I track him down.

The facts come together in a rush. Everything I have gleaned from that county has always been interconnected. X's great-grandfather and grandfather are buried at the cemetery across from St. Peter's—the cemetery just south of the landfill and just north of the place where I picked through creek detritus to find pieces of the past I could possess. That cemetery never belonged to St. Peter's. It's always been a city cemetery. I just didn't know.

§

So who have I really cursed, in the end? Surely not the girls who no longer troop into The Plaza to buy clothes; they order online now, their reinventions directly shipped from a world that will accept them if Pitt County does not. When I was a girl in Greenville, there was no internet, no new space. But the fact is that, in the years since I've left, Greenville has doubled over and stood back up with twice the weight in its populous belly, growing massive and mighty. The town is bloated with newcomers, Evanses loading up the census rolls until no one can tell who is one of Those Evanses unless they dig. The town swelled, the county swelled, draining pocosins in the outskirted tobacco fields to claim land for new developments.

The joke is not the fact that there is a cemetery outside a dead mall. The joke is not that the mall must be haunted. The joke is on me for imagining that an ancestral history in Pitt County would have allowed me to transform from a yearning adolescent into a woman who securely knew where she belonged. Of course I know where I belong. Yet I'm still jealously whittling facts into daggers, obsessing about a place paved over by a history I could not sink my claws into. I could rip out all my teeth, break off my finger bones joint by joint, and jackhammer a hole so I could bury my DNA beside the blurring marble headstones, but the acidic Pitt County soil dissolves calcium within twenty years. Cement covers those decaying coffins in the old Plaza parking lot, ensuring their perpetual stake on the land. The Evanses have a permanence in Pitt County that will not erode even if the mall is razed. And here I am: still peering over the wall, clutching coins for Charon, wanting to buy my way in.

Mädchenfänger

1. **The best friend** is dead, and you are relieved.

2. **You find her** age, twenty-nine, to be certain it is her before you are ashamed for feeling relieved.

3. **She has not startled you** in years; it has been eighteen since she first slipped a favor on your finger, *let's play a game.*

4. **You were just grateful** she did not steal your diary like the other girls had.

5. **You remember** the messages on your answering machine after two grades of bestfriendship, the mortifying hurt as she demoted you, loser.

6. **You tried to leave** breadcrumbs so she would follow you back into childhood, but she narrowed her eyes, dropping her lunch tray to pursue the yellow pills pockmarking a cottage she would consume.

7. **A mechanism of preservation**, choosing to remember the nightmarish years instead of the ones when she had pulled out her trundle bed for you.

8. **Now the clock has stopped**, the battery gone out, and you feel the noose on your neck.

9. **Not your neck**, but your finger, the one that dialed her phone number hundreds of times.

10. **The first finger** trap was called a Mädchenfänger—girl catcher—and the unsuspecting party named a victim.

11. **The trap** is best known as a child's prank, but the finger trap's design has been used in surgeries to immobilize an injury.

12. **After you had both become adults**, she called you, twice, on phone numbers you never gave her.

13. **Your movements** were panicked, rabbit-in-a-net, a pullback throttled by your hunger for her friendship.

14. **Forgiveness** was what she wanted, but you did not trust her; it felt like that old trick, another girl listening on the other phone and waiting to pounce on your half lie.

15. **A part** that pulled you apart when you found out she was dead was that you were not **a part**.

16. A part of her death was removal, no confessor left to release your ungranted **forgiveness**.

17. You stretched toward a guiltless future, but the strangle constricted **your movements**.

18. You had relied on a girl's behavior to strengthen the rightness of your hurt, the old pain to deepen your pain, long **after you had both become adults**.

19. You tried to bend backwards, thinking the years had grown you far enough apart, but the knot tightened to catch you, **the trap.**

20. A safety net, a reminder of the adolescence when she still clutched you, a tether you could not snip off **the first finger.**

21. Your throat compressed as she grew beyond you, your breath shallowed with her voice, sure she would finally cut the remember-string tied around her knuckle, **not your neck.**

22. But she did not, and **now the clock has stopped.**

23. She reached for you and you leaned back, **a mechanism of preservation.**

24. You could not know you were ensnared until **you tried to leave.**

25. But you did not try to leave—that, **you remember.**

26. You slid the trap onto your finger like a fool, **you were just grateful.**

27. When she died, the plait sucked tight like a vacuum, a phantom pull you welcomed; **she has not startled you.**

28. You did not realize that to loosen the chokehold, two people must move closer together; you beckon with a bamboo braid wedged on your digit, a long-fingered crone calling out *let's play a game*, but **you cannot find her.**

29. You trace the Mädchenfänger's three-stranded weave.

30. The best friend is dead and you are relieved

> you were not **the best friend**
> you were not **the best friend**
> you were not **the best friend.**

She'll Only Come
Out at Night

Our guts churned as Shelly dared us into a game of "Who's Got the Nerve to Hit Me" on those viscous, smothered summer nights at the park behind our neighborhood, our parents encased in our air-conditioned houses, watching Friday night family programming beside our siblings on the couch. But we melted out our front doors and swiped our kickstands with our insteps and the yellow streetlight streamed off our exposed shoulder blades as we cut swathes through the swelter, merging, drawn together to the park. We didn't underdog on the swings, pretending to be children, or climb on top of the soccer goals like the boys would; we weren't lured by the tobacco fields on the other side of the broken wooden fence in the way they'd called to us in the daylight. We met right at the front of the park, visible to anyone who had the guts to join us, anyone who might have the guts to follow our instantaneous desire to actually hit Shelly in the face when she dared us.

We all wanted to do it. We all disliked her, disliked how mean she was, how unafraid. We disliked the bleach streak in the ponytail she sleeked back to expose her sharply featured, hawk-like face; we disliked her father, whom we feared as she invoked his orders to elbow aside her disinterest in cheerleading, invoked his pride in her for doing boyish things. We feared Shelly as she pushed us all out of the way on the basketball court, played harder, shot harder, as she slammed home runs like a boy, wore T-shirts untucked like a boy, talked back to the teachers like a boy. She was mean but she was one of us; no one would punch her, no one would slap her, no one would say anything mean to her face. And she knew it.

So she scowled and narrowed her eyes with pleasure and we collected behind her as Shelly strode away from the park, right down the center of the darkened street, and we were pumping our fists in the air and yell-singing Shelly's lyrical twist, *SLAM, duh-duh-duh, duh-duh-duh, LET THE GIRLS BE GIRLS* because we weren't boys, we didn't want to be boys, we would never have sung *LET THE GIRLS BE BOYS*. Who wanted to be a boy, all that visible desire poking pleats into their khaki shorts, sweaty and slapping tennis balls against the gym wall before school, the endless dirty rhymes they made from each other's names? Who wanted to be a boy? We were girls, unbent, belligerent, say-it-to-my-fucking-face girls, though under the fluorescence of eighth grade we were soft, secret, clenching our right fists under the demure cover of our yin-yang-ringed left hands, low in our laps beneath the lab tables, hiss-whispering about Shelly Rucker, smelly fucker. But we would meet her at the park when the cicadas shrilled into the thick night quilt, the husks of our guts burning with the things we hadn't done. She knew that too.

Creepsake

: a memento growing along a wall, like a vine
I left things behind, fetishes tied around the fences I wanted to infiltrate. I pushed my copy of *The Baby-Sitters Club: Super Special #1* under the dust ruffle of Heather's bed after a sleepover. I waited for her to tell me to come back. I would have noticed anything she had forgotten. But the only item left between the cracks of my pre-adolescence was Joanne's copy of *The Wind in the Willows*, inexplicably signed by the local kid who had starred in a TGIF sitcom. It was a token I kept long after I rejected Joanne's too-easily-gained friendship, hoping the kid's autograph would be valuable someday. It was not. I thought my "misplaced" belongings would be magnets, inexorably pulling relationships back to me, bound to return that last piece of connection out of obligation. They did not.

: a memento obtained by moving slowly
The "Remember DQ!" bumper sticker. The cafeteria fork and knife I slid into my backpack. The dusty soda bottles

I collected on my dresser top. The Facebook notification emails, proof I had been on the receiving end, once.

: a memento presented after sneaking up behind someone
I cashed in my savings bonds—the $100 I won at the statewide spelling bee in second grade, the $50 my god-mother gave me for First Communion, the odd $25 bonds from the day I was born. While none of them had fully matured, I netted enough to cover my half of the plane ticket in the deal I struck with my parents, sending me back to Oregon for spring break. I had been writing histrionic letters of homesickness to my friends during the previous two years, and I telephoned them all, ex-hilarated to announce my return, to book hangouts and sleepovers. Long-distance calls still cost ten cents a min-ute, and I assumed that was why they were surprised to hear my voice.

There was a platitude I relied on—*when we get back together, it's like no time has passed*—as I invaded their bedrooms that spring break, afternoon after afternoon. I had left as a ten-year-old and I'd come back in the thick of middle school; all my friends' new alliances with girls from elementary schools I didn't know made me bitterly, bitterly jealous. I couldn't get caught up on two years' worth of gossip, but I could make an appearance at the middle school I would have attended, twinning Marin's schedule for an entire day, wearing the fabric-painted "Three Girls in Oregon are My Best Friends" T-shirt I was given at my going-away party, nearly threadbare because I'd worn it regularly, reminding everyone in North Carolina that their friendship was unnecessary. I wasted one of my days of spring break going to school, but I believed it was worth it to prove that I wasn't permanently gone, although I was most assuredly permanently gone, the house sold, my father's degree obtained, the assistantship expired.

Karyn turned around in English several times, like she was trying to place me. I wanted to scream, *Your mom was my third-grade teacher! We were in Campfire Girls together! I lost a $20 bill in the woods behind your house and we spent all afternoon looking for it!* but there was something in her absent gaze that balled in the pit of my stomach. Karyn didn't recognize me. She pitied the girl she'd seen eagerly trotting behind Marin in the hall, shadowing someone she used to know.

I returned to Oregon five more times, with my family, with my boyfriend, with my children, retracing the path I used to walk to school, stopping in front of my old house and staring at the places I used to belong. I drove by the houses of my old friends. One time I saw my friend's mother working in the front yard and my parents stopped the rental car so I could run up and say hello. My friend's mother could not place me either—I was out of context, unexpected—but she pretended she knew me. I wanted to yell, *I'm in a photograph of your daughter's ninth birthday party, sitting on the stairs right inside the door! I used to dangle on your backyard swing set as your daughter and I described our fantasy husbands!*

I have a glass perfume bottle she brought me back from Egypt sitting on my dresser on the other side of the country! but I just said to my friend's mother, "Well, tell her that I stopped by to say hi," only realizing later how ominous and foreboding and frightening that must have sounded from some girl her daughter once knew, out of her life, trying to prove she could get back in.

: a memento of intrusion into someone else's photograph
My family stopped to visit another family on another trip back—we had known each other from church. I'd gone to their house after Mass and helped pick apples from the tree in the front yard. The mother urged me to go in and wake up her daughter, who was napping in the family room—everyone was convinced it would be The Surprise of the Century. I followed the mother into the darkened room and the mother shook her daughter awake, "Wake up, you'll never guess who's here." The daughter sat up and looked at me, confused, and I said "Hi," as the moment fell flat on its face. I never really knew the girl, only went to her house once or twice. The daughter was a quick study and threw on a pretend-surprised face, but it was the first time I considered that this wasn't such a great idea.

I looked up the daughter six years later and found that she was running a vineyard. I thought about ordering wine from her for my wedding, justifying that it wasn't such a big vineyard, she probably handled the orders, there was a chance she would recognize my name. And then what?

One old friend was an opera singer; another was married, Mormon, and lost. So many lost. I searched again and again for my elementary school crush of four years, and for Marin. I found no online trace of them past their senior year of high school, which frustrated me.

I sent a feeler message through MySpace to another old friend, thirteen years after I'd moved away, asking if she was the same girl who had attended my elementary school. My old friend responded affirmatively, and I sent her a complete update on my life since 1992. She never wrote back. I didn't know what I'd done wrong.

A friend-for-two-weeks from summer camp whom I found on social media, six years later, was living with the boy about whom she had written in one of her two post-camp letters to me—she'd had an unbearable crush on the boy during camp. I sent her a message, informing her that I had a letter she'd written about her current boyfriend, and I'd be happy to mail it if she'd give me her address. She replied, and I sent the letter, but I never heard from her again.

I left behind a digital trail like a slug oozing slime: incandescent in the light, but something no one wanted to touch.

: a memento of the gradual, permanent deformation produced by a continued application of stress

My yearbooks are always within reach. I type names into search engines, I find unprotected Facebook profiles and I follow their Friends lists to silently connect the faces of the ones I knew, the ones who know each other still. They don't see me tucking away the memory of a bond, that little creepsake no one noticed was missing.

Not Something That's Gone

All italicized and bolded portions of this essay are repurposed from Cat's Eye *by Margaret Atwood.*

I'm light-headed, as if convalescing, finding one more truth I'd forgotten that I'd forgotten in the narrative within the narrative: *I've been prepared for almost anything except absence.*

You are dead, a fact that still stomach-punches me as hard as that fall afternoon when I was doing the rounds, keeping tabs on your location, keeping you in place. And I am still as nervous-sick as I was when we were girls, anticipating your phone calls, dreading your phone calls, hiding the content of your phone calls from my parents and myself. I was twelve and I was twenty-nine, crying myself to sleep, irreversibly done with waiting to be found.

321–1168. My fingers move across an invisible keypad, a burnt neural pathway from the days before cell phones, reflexively drumming a tense rhythm, counting down, but it would be useless to dial a number you have not answered for years. I finally want you to call me; I finally want to answer.

I can close my eyes and see the white hum of light dawning outside your plantation-shuttered blinds. I'm light limbed, sliding silently from my side of your full-size bed to sit on the carpet beside the grow lamps, quietly removing the CD booklet from "Dookie" to read the lyrics I was supposed to already know, listening to your even breathing, afraid to go downstairs without you, afraid to wake you up. I want you awake and I want you dead. I want you to never know what I am doing and I want you to interrupt me. I want you twelve years old and I want you thirty-seven, but I would take you thirty, the age you never reached. More than anything, I want to stop seeing you everywhere and in everything: Stone Temple Pilots on the radio, the black-and-white beaded bracelet you re-gifted to me, incense, Puma sneakers, "Saturday Night Live": I don't want to stop seeing you everywhere because it is the only way I will ever see you again.

I am waiting, because twice I have animated you into action through the electric thread invisibly connecting us; twice I began to write about you and twice you called me, out of the blue as I remained silent on the other end, receiving the shock, welcoming it. You are dead, you are dead, the online obituary says you have been gone nine years, but I stare at the trail of detritus you left behind when you evaporated from this earth: salt packets, Winterfresh wrappers, vanilla cupcake batter, a muddy river. If I stare long enough, the path begins to narrow into the pupil of Margaret Atwood's cat's eye, compressing and entwining fiction and nonfiction. I try to distinguish her words from mine by emboldening and italicizing, but the twinned narrative remains, strewn with **orange Popsicles, penny gumballs, red licorice, gnawed hair, dirty ice.**

———

I put on my new dress, but I've misjudged, based on the other fifth-grade girls who are all clad in Duck Head shorts this spring. Floral dresses were popular two thousand miles away in my old home, snuggled in the fold of the Willamette Valley, but the splayed coastal plains of North Carolina offer nowhere to hide. These girls surround me in their purple and red shorts, a duck head sewn above the buttons on their left butt cheeks, one blank eye staring.

I have underestimated them all year. In the fall, two girls befriended me, but within three months they had stolen my diary. Bewildered, I retreated toward the other newcomer— you. Neither of us is from this up-jumped, third-tier university town of good ol' boys, outskirted with tobacco fields, infielded with skinny eighty-foot pines trapping down the yellow-pollen air, honeying our lungs and sticking like cigarette tar. Neither of us grew up tubing the sluggish milky-brown river that twines past hog farms, picking up pig shit and entrails, sliding over flat fields in a shallow bed. The official, cautionary motto in this deeply racially divided town: Find Yourself in Good Company.

You don't appear in my reclaimed diary until April, though we've been in the same classroom all year, our houses in the same neighborhood all along. You're from Indiana, and I was born in Indiana, a fact I exploit to cement our friendship. You long for the life you recently left, and I'm willing to adopt a homesickness for a place I barely remember. We start a club, with a membership of two, calling it IWIWII: I Wish I Was in Indiana. It's the glue that bonds us, as temporary as Elmer's, though we smear it on our hearts anyway, smashing ourselves together, best-friending into our own Red Rover team, daring the others to break us apart.

It seems impossible we'll end up where we end up by seventh grade, two years later, as you elbow me in the hall and place your three-ring binder from physical science in my hands, more delicate than you've been with me all year, whispering, "Be careful! There's a roach in the back pocket." I follow orders, though I don't understand. Your science fair project is "The Effects of Alcohol on Animals," a suggestion from Hannah, one of your brother's friends, an eighteen-year-old "bitch" with long brown hair who "lives in a big-ass house" near Bath. I haven't met Hannah because I'm "too goody-goody." Hannah hates goody-goodies. Hannah is a phantom of cool, and I'm so jealous I want to rip her teeth out, so I am relieved when I bristle at one of your commands and you declare, surprised and proud, "You're a bitch just like Hannah!"

You aren't able to complete the science project because one of your hamsters dies of alcohol poisoning, but it's all right—you were tired of taking care of them, and if they hadn't died you were going to leave the cage open for your cat. "At least I tried some of the sample," you barked in your dry-skin monotone, smirking. But you still had to turn something in, so your distracted and harried parents paid for a classroom of your own, grow lights hanging over a tray of carefully saved seeds and stems beside your bed, the contrasting **smell of old wood, furniture polish; formaldehyde and dead mice.**

———

I wake late, roll to my side and stuff my ragged yellow baby blanket to the bottom of my sleeping bag so you will not know I smuggled it along when you wake up. You will wake up soon.

The breathless sprint of adolescence has not begun. We are still in the thrall of our childhood during the summer before sixth grade, crusty kneed and carelessly wearing old softball-team T-shirts, standing on the two-by-four my dad drilled into a swing, our hands on the soft blue-and-white rope, leaping off a rusted metal seat as we catapult beneath the pines, the needles a silent cushion.

There is a girl from our class who lives a block away, but we don't invite her over; we're repulsed by the bologna smell of her house and the merriness of her plump cheeks and the way no one else talks to her at school. We live in a well-curated zoo of children our age. Both of the school buses servicing our neighborhood had been so crammed, we'd sat three to a seat as we were cargoed away from our white-bread suburban neighborhood to our elementary school in the heart of a Black neighborhood to desegregate the public schools. This was 1993. There was a rusted eight-foot-high chain-link fence separating our schoolyard from the nearby shotgun houses that looked like we could take a knife and slice them down the center, two even halves falling away. We derided the inhabitants as being so poor they probably couldn't afford toilet paper. "Sorry, kids, it's another pine cone night," we crowed, leaning against the brown pleather seats, laughter streaming from our eyes as our Black bus driver caravaned us back to Club Pines.

All our neighborhood classmates are preparing for cotillion in the fall. You and I did not grow up with this one-hand-delicately-pressed-to-the-chest tradition, and so we mock the inanity of learning to jitterbug and waltz, though since I have begun reading "Gone with the Wind," I secretly daydream of dancing with boys. But you fall prey to the pressures of your parents one last time and quietly admit to me, the week before cotillion begins, that you're going after all. I have been outclassed and outboxed.

We invent a Backyard Bonanza, featuring the acrobatic tricks we will perform on the swing, publicizing our show by scrawling the details on a huge piece of plywood we find in my dad's woodworking pile. We believe someone will come to watch us, someone will come to claim us. We forget that we are midwesterners in the South, hayseeds spilling from the upturned cuffs of our jean shorts onto acidic soil; nothing will root, nothing will sprout.

The bologna girl appears in my backyard, drawn by our advertisement, and as much as we try to wish her away, to magnetize the popular girls instead, she is the only one who shows up, clapping like a seal, eager to please. We sigh, because **whatever category we are in also includes her.**

———

In the corner of a parking lot, I have halted my minivan, rolled the windows down, and closed my eyes as my daughters chatter in the back seats. I am trying to parse apart which repressed sense has reactivated, started this storm stirring up memories resting on the bottom of the sea and put them back into my photic zone, floating and sifting.

It is the scent of maple syrup under the breezeway near our middle school cafeteria; the cheap smell of thick, creamsicle-colored samples of hair gunk that we'd snagged and smeared into our ponytails (we laughed as we put on our swimsuits and showered together, shampooing it out with strawberry Alberto VO5); the sickly sweet flush of Caribbean Cool Teen Spirit emanating from my newly shaved armpits as I smuggled a rainbow star-shaped pin out of the dollar store. The cool smooth tops of Lender's Bagelettes. Orange dusty powder and the thin, crinkly plastic of Andy Capp's Hot Fries. My blocked ears open and I hear the gentle guitar strumming at the beginning of "All Apologies." I see a girl with frizzing blond hair and dark eyebrows wearing a black-and-white-checked flannel shirt and jean shorts, impatiently waiting.

I dreamed about you last night. We were in a park and we were adults, remembering an incident that never actually happened; remembering how, as teens, a man had once tried to get all three of us (there was another girl, Gretchen?) to go with him to Florida, but you and I had run away from him into that very same park, into the smell of hyssop drenched with evening dew, laughing at the absurdity of his offer. I was trying to make you remember the nonexistent event, pointing out the trail we had run along, the flowers still growing, ancestral remnants from fifteen-odd years earlier, but you just looked at me and silently shook your head, disavowing what I knew; you were not there, it did not happen like that.

I questioned if you had briefly forgotten the incident or if I was remembering the story wrong and for some reason you couldn't speak to correct me, but in my dream, I was just struck by how sad it was that we had shared something real and significant and I was the only one to remember it. I suppose all three are accurate: you do not remember it, you cannot correct me, and I am the only one left to remember anything we shared.

In waking life, I wondered at the vividness of what I had conjured, at the specificity—Florida, of all places—and the distinctive scent of damp hyssop as we rejected his offer, together. When I looked up the floral language of hyssop, I found two meanings: external truth and purification. There was no Florida, there was no hyssop, and there were no teen years together. There is no you to corroborate or contradict me anymore. But **the flowers, the smell, the movement of the leaves persist, rich, mesmerizing, desolating, infused with grief.**

I continue east, riding my bike no-hands-on-the-handlebars through the pine-lined streets to your house. I find an unexpected freedom in your stilted formal dining room with the mahogany table set for twelve, the living room with chintz-covered armchairs and your sister's huge senior portrait oil-painted and hanging above the unused fireplace; a freedom unlike anything in my sibling-cluttered, sawdust-projected, aspirational-living house. Your house is prepared for a magazine-perfect life, but no one lives there. Your sister is out dating boyfriends and egging mailboxes when she gets angry; your brother waxes his surfboard and drives an hour to the beach, making friends on the sand and crashing on someone's moldy living room carpet; your parents decide Staccato is where the glitterati of our town gather and so they leave us to our own devices as they sweep down the staircase, a floral whisper of your mom's perfume lingering as she brushes by me, standing in the entry hall clutching my sleeping bag, astonished.

We are only eleven, still children, longing for what is leaving. You put on your old "Sesame Street" Christmas cassette and we sing Christmas songs in the summer, yanking Egg Beaters out of the fridge as you lead me through the process of making vanilla cupcakes from scratch, batter we eat before they can bake. I am exhilarated by the misbehavior no one will arrest. No one is watching.

Except you believe someone is watching, a girl next door whose friendship you had accepted and quickly rejected, a

smudge of a girl who tried to befriend you by reusing a nickname your old best friend in Indiana had called you. You're
sure she is jealously watching us through the side window
that looks directly into your living room, so we taunt her by
walking like an Egyptian, leaping through the air, anything to
make us laugh and make her realize she is not included.

I will not make her mistake. We create another club called
ALESS: Against four girls whose names I don't need to mention; either you remember them or you don't. We invent
nicknames for ourselves: you are Bañana, and I am Kiwi. We
studiously design symbols as signatures for our daily notes
to each other—yours is a spiral with a line connecting the
innermost endpoint to the outermost as a pathway out of the
maze, and mine is a perversion of the pi symbol with a diagonal top line, jaunty but derivative.

We stay up to watch Nirvana on "Saturday Night Live"
with your brother. I don't understand any of the skits and I
don't think they're funny because I'm not an adult, but I'm
trying. We ride our bikes to McDonald's and stuff our pockets with salt packets. You have decided we are going to salt
the Smudge's yard, killing the grass by smothering it with
damage that won't appear for weeks. We crack the packets
into a bowl, disappointed by the small handful of salt we have
gathered, and wait until 10 p.m. to "take a walk." We pace in
front of her yard two separate times, feinting our throws,
nervous by her bright porch light. Eventually, either you or I
quietly release a handful on her yard, near the curb, and we
run inside your house.

When I tell this story in the years to come, we will have
had canisters full of Morton's, and we will have danced across

the yard, sprinkling hatred everywhere. There is the truth, which only you and I know, but it is not bombastic enough.

By the time your parents get home, we have already committed our sins, already eaten all of the cupcake batter. You leave the unwashed bowl in the sink, evidence they will not mention, though you want them to.

We sleep at your house through sixth grade, moving toward seventh, various sugars sweetening the gall of outgrowing girlhood. **Some nights we have marshmallows, for a treat.**

———

There are several diseases of the memory, which is why I invent a rivalry with the girl who moves into a house near yours the summer before we begin seventh grade. She has the same initials as a girl I knew in Oregon, so I collide them together, insisting that I KNOW HER, this new girl who's shown up. It's a reincarnation neither you nor I believe, but it's interesting enough to give us someone new to resent. We call her out from her house one night, and her little brothers and sisters straggle behind us into the street. We've decided I'm going to race her. It's a way of showing off, a pissing contest for girls: I'm going to race her and I'm going to beat her.

But she beats me—by a decent margin too—and I can barely stand the humiliation. You approach the new girl as I fake a limp, winded, and you ask Gretchen if she wants to hang out. We turn into three that night, but I don't realize we will actually remain a two-set; one will be left, dangling, pretending to tie a sneaker with IWIWII in blue Bic on the sole, rubbing off.

The humidity is so thick it gets inside my veins, stiffens my resolve to hold on to what is mine. Later that month, I convince you that we need to give Gretchen a test if she wants to join ALESS and hate girls she has never met, so we literally write up an exam on loose-leaf, asking obscure questions about both ourselves and the girls in ALESS. You feed Gretchen the correct answers, unbeknownst to me, and when she passes the test, you write me a note: "Hey Co-President, we have done basically nothing all year. What was the point of us?" **My eyes are open but I'm not there. I'm off to the side.**

———

In late morning the phone wakes me. There are calls to my family's answering machine when you know we're at church, messages that drawl over the tape as I perch on the edge of my parents' bed, ready to erase your voice when you finally stop talking. There are calls I take in the front yard, nervously trying to recite the lyrics to "All Apologies" since you'd made me declare a favorite Nirvana song, accidentally calling the ashes of her enemy "the ashes of heredity." There are calls where I call-wait between you and Gretchen, mediating an argument about shoes, whether Gretchen should be allowed to get Simples or if she should get Pumas because you already got Simples, calls that end when I can hear Gretchen's voice on the other end of the wrong line and she has to go, you have to go. I stay in the front yard, pacing, holding the receiver cradled against my face, pretending to talk, too ashamed to return inside. When you call, I answer. When you don't call, I wait to answer.

You make alliances with Gretchen at school, purposefully within my earshot, plans I will assume I am invited to join; I will overhear and bike over after school and ring Gretchen's doorbell and when her mother answers, I will confidently say hello and walk upstairs but when I open the door to Gretchen's room, you two are sprawled on the floor paging through the seventh-grade yearbook, laughing, looking up, startled, frowning.

I will look at that yearbook I had vandalized by writing near your photo, illegibly, "Someone on this page is a witch with a B," and I will be dumbfounded to discover that you have re-defaced the yearbook on my page with a long screed listing my faults. The one that will cling to my chest like a leech is that I have pita-bread breasts, a truth I will never grow beyond, a description that haunts me for decades.

We devolve into passive aggression in eighth grade. You eat lunch with me because we have to eat together—we've been identified together for so long that no one cares enough to try to befriend one or the other; we are not separate people. You condescend to speak to me as little as possible and only when no one is looking. I don't understand what I did. You swallow these little yellow pills with a "V" in the center that you call M&Ms and I think they are an allergy medication until I remember you aren't allergic to anything.

You accuse me of being a narc. I don't know what a narc is, but I know if I won't tell you my locker combination, I'll confirm your suspicions. And I know I can't tell you that I don't know what you're talking about, with narcs and M&Ms. Once, I make the mistake of asking what a bong is. You glare at me, cup your right hand and smack it against your left shoulder four times, imitating the disabled kids, "DUH, bitch." I don't ask again.

You call me, corroborating that I haven't been talking to anyone about you. "I can't have you doing that. I don't want to have to send someone to take care of you," you warn, and though years later it will sound like a terribly trite, "Godfather"-ish warning that a thirteen-year-old upper-middle-class white girl would have never mustered the resources to carry out, at the time it is as real as the time you pushed your smudge of a neighbor off the curb, calling it yours. I'm light headed at your call, reeling, innocent, but I might as well be guilty because I have dreamed of refusing to be your alibi when your mom calls. The sick fear of misbehaving so badly that you will finally leave me alone both attracts and repels me. I want this rotten friendship to be cored, one way or another, because you will send someone to take care of me. It will not be you.

Every whisper I see you mock-cover with your hand when you and Gretchen pass me in the hall is about my pita-bread breasts, I am certain. Every after-school hangout with Gretchen that you theatrically plan in a loud voice involves getting a ride to Bath and hanging out with Hannah, my replacement. After a time, training my eyes not to meet yours lest I betray my fear, my longing, my hurt, I begin to avoid you, which only sparks your interest. You call me and mock my cheap blue flannel shirt, my knock-off Birkenstocks, "What did you say your favorite Grateful Dead song was?" certain I know nothing, brutal insults I endure, though **I hardly hear them any more because I hardly listen.**

———

I write you notes, including sticks of Winterfresh gum, because that is how I curry your friendship now. I remember your disappointment when I'd handed you a note between keyboarding and science and you shook out my complicated note folds, looking for gum, astonished that I would try to give you something as useless as my thoughts without including payment. I think you will write me back, calling me Kiwi, plotting a hate crime we should commit against someone on the ALESS roster, or your neighbor, or Gretchen.

For a long time, **this would make me feel more ordinary.**

But instead you slyly ask for my backpack during social studies, rifling through it as you sit in the row behind me, beside the popular stoner boys, removing mechanical pencils and my Bulldog Bucks, handing my backpack back to me, laughing, my possessions now yours. It is a silent transaction I am too stunned to question, though when you ask again for my backpack the next day, I only remove my Dr Pepper Lip Smacker first, leaving a half-used pack of Winterfresh as a reward, a bribe, because I know you need to exact something.

———

There's your face again, a blurred reflection of a moon, behind the front window of my old house, my current house, all the houses I lived in during college, all the places you have followed me, all the places I waited to see you again. There's your face on a website supporting Ron Paul; you're twenty-six. There's your twelve-year-old face, smirking at my mother while she held the camera. If I had known I owned five photographs in which you appear, I'd have ripped them up years ago. You look like a peripheral friend because you mostly appear in group shots. We are touching in none of them. There is only one photo of the two of us alone, together: it is my twelfth birthday party and I am wrapping your body in toilet paper. I stand behind you, my eyes trained on the roll of toilet paper I am holding. Your eyes are bound and you look like a soldier from World War II who has lost both of her eyes. One arm is sloppily wrapped, but you hold it out, waiting. Your lips are slightly parted, a sarcastic expression.

The other photographs I see of you are stolen from websites, from your Facebook profile—a profile I never bring myself to friend-request. In one image, you hold a puppy, and your gray-blue eyes are clear. In a photograph from your second wedding, you are looking radiantly at your new husband; your hair is down and straight and your waist is bigger than I expected. You are in a barn with your husband, holding your youngest son. In the final photo, your youngest is wearing a onesie calling you a fox, and you captioned it, "Still 10 more pregnancy pounds to go!"

I had trained myself to only remember your preteenage disaffect, your dry-skinned forearms perpetually crossed, bored and unsatisfied as I bounded towards you in the hall between classes, yet I am confronted with your age-softened smile, your unarmored emotion, barely a hint of the girl I knew. But I find you again in your business school graduation photo, the way you face the camera, the lack of a smile; you look serious, so serious, not a hint of sarcasm playing on the corners of your lips. Every other graduate is smiling in their composite shot, but not you. You are unamused, you do not concede.

I shudder, grateful for the consistency, the justification, the reminder, and carry that version of you with me as *I walk west.*

———

We fall together onto the floor, Gretchen and I, dumped, left behind when your father gets promoted to a position in the suburbs of Chicago and you move abruptly over Christmas break, sketching out vague details because it isn't important we know why you're going, where you're going, only that you will leave me waiting, unsure the end has actually come. I crawl toward Gretchen hesitantly, afraid she will report my behavior to you, but she reaches out a hand and helps me up.

For the rest of eighth grade, Gretchen and I decorate each other's lockers and play basketball on the school team and sit side by side in the clarinet row. Gretchen modifies a pair of blue corduroys we thrifted into a skirt I plan to wear, along with a gray baby doll T-shirt and my mom's real Birkenstocks, to Brittany and Taylor's birthday party—all fashion statements I couldn't make when you were around to mock me, remind me of my place; who was I trying to be?

I accompany Gretchen to a youth dance and her youth group leader is kind enough to ask me to dance. It is my first dance with a boy, though he is in his midtwenties, like a kindly older brother, very careful to keep his hands friendly and light. I am aware that I am not sexualized—"pita-bread breasts" floats into my head, unbidden—and it is embarrassing, especially as Gretchen slow-dances with her thirteen-year-old semiboyfriend across the room. I am grateful you are not there to see, grateful I am there with Gretchen and you are not.

Near the end of the school year, after Gretchen and I have already submitted our secretly coded Beatles-freak messages to each other for publication in the yearbook, you show up in my algebra class. The lights are off and we're watching a movie and out of the corner of my eye you glide into view, streaming between the desks, to nab your tessellation of Grateful Dead bears off the wall. I can barely breathe because you are a ghost, a ghost who was supposed to stay dead. You stand at the front of the classroom with our teacher and talk for a couple of minutes and I see you scanning the room until you make eye contact with me and you smirk and I know everything I have done will be undone, everything that has been real has been a mirage; you are back and you will claim what is yours and nothing can prevent you from returning again and again. You were dead and you are alive again. I am nothing but *bargain clothes and wrenches.*

———

Underneath its arm, wrapped in a white cloth, is Cordelia's head.

The marble twists when, as a senior in high school, I read Margaret Atwood's roman à clef "Cat's Eye," a novel reeking of Margaret's personal knowledge. There are details I suss out repeatedly in Margaret's body of work, vivid descriptions that convince me "fiction" is nothing but truth twisted a tad to force a conclusion the author couldn't attain in real life. When Margaret describes Elaine peeling the cool, mushroomy bottoms of her feet at night, an act of self-mutilation during her preadolescent torment at the hands of her "friends," I know that she knows. When "Elaine" remembers *the same shame, the sick feeling in my body, the same knowledge of my own wrongness*, I know that she knows.

I scribble memories in the margins when I'm supposed to be taking notes on the arc of the book. I cannot handle the similarities: Elaine, the protagonist, moves to a new town and meets Cordelia when she is nine; Cordelia is her best friend until she is her best tormentor, debasing Elaine by ring-leading their friends into girlhood cruelties that leave Elaine shaken, terrified, desperate to prove that she is still worthy of being Cordelia's friend. I want to feel comforted that someone else has experienced the kind of shame I felt, but I am humiliated that it was known.

It alarms me that after their preadolescence, Cordelia reappears in Elaine's life three times, but it also consoles me to have a blueprint. First, Cordelia falls apart in high school, seeking Elaine's friendship—and the power balance shifts. Next, Cordelia puts herself back together as a twenty-something and makes a point of seeking out Elaine to show her that she is living just fine. Finally, Cordelia ends up in a mental hospital and asks Elaine to get her out. Elaine refuses but is plagued by dreams of Cordelia's constant presence. Elaine finally sends a letter to the hospital, but it comes back Address Unknown and Elaine knows Cordelia is out there, somewhere, angry with her.

I know where you are; at least, I believe I do. You live outside Chicago, until I receive a phone call during my sophomore year of high school. Eight months after you left North Carolina, my family had moved too and so I am living in Indiana again after all, three hours south of you in a town that leans against the state border of Illinois, longingly.

My mother hands me the cordless phone, saying your name, and it hits me in the chest like a punch, knocking out my breath as my head lightens, dizzy, out of practice, forgetting. I hold the receiver to my ear and hear your low, dry, midwestern rasp as you say, "I got your phone number from Gretchen," and I scurry up to my bedroom, unsure what I may need to hide.

I retrogress into my old shock-absorber position so quickly that I am neither surprised that you have contacted me nor astonished that you are now, actually, only living an hour away from me outside Indianapolis with your mother, who has left your father. I realize I have been waiting for you to emerge again. We both Wished We Were in Indiana and here we are.

You begin to apologize for "the way you were" in middle school; you tell me you flushed the last of your drugs because "there was no point anymore" but I am dazed, unable to determine what the point was in the first place. You are as forgetful as Cordelia, as eager to remember things differently, and I am eager to forget them too, but I am wary of your apology. It comes too easily, too unearned; I had dreamed of extracting it from you like a splinter, painful until it was out; only then could we both forget it had ever happened.

So when you tell me your mother wants to speak to mine, I know I was right to mistrust your contrition—somehow I have been implicated, somehow I will be punished for something you have done. But I warily obey and lope downstairs, handing the phone to my mother.

I watch my mother's expression as I overhear your mother's voice on the other end of the line, proposing that you and I meet at a mall near your town. The way it is being arranged is alarming because you and I are fifteen, after all, not toddlers who need to be grouped into a playdate. But your mother is desperate to connect us, and my mother is perplexed at my reticence as she holds her thumb over the speaker, probing, "I thought you two were still friends?" I cannot answer that question; I invent an illogical excuse and my mother tells yours that weekend won't work, proposes we find another weekend down the line, an arrangement that never comes to fruition because I "forget" to return your call. Believing the first exhibition is over, *I leave the gallery.*

———

At which I dare not look because it is easier to blur the lines of the narrative into a convenient truth: I do not stare directly at our friendship but amplify the glare of my isolation and your part in it. I start to lose touch with the real events. The constructions take over. I neglect to mention that we were still writing notes to each other into seventh grade, even as you began to prefer Gretchen, to confide only in Gretchen. I forget that Gretchen was never cruel to me; Gretchen was always kind, Gretchen was your friend but she was my friend too, throughout seventh grade, throughout eighth grade, reliable. It is easier to forget how your notes made me snicker, even now; easier to remember them as jibes barbed with malice rather than inside jokes we'd once shared.

Your move to Indianapolis did not last long. You graduated from the high school in Illinois. It was easier to ignore the upheaval and inconsistency that must have rattled you and focus, instead, on the role I needed you to fill as the cause of my pain, that cherished, tender bruise I'd slam against a corner when it started to yellow. You provided an explanation for my adolescent distrust, my wall-building: you did this to me.

I wanted a picture when I wrote about you in college even though the portrait in my head was indelible, your blue eyes in that sarcastic squint, the right corners of your thin lips turning up in a sneer, your frizzing blond hair pulled back in a ponytail, your dark eyebrows contrasting, ready to bend, breaking my heart with your disregard. But I packed no photos with me when I moved to the dorms, and so you remained transient, a ghost, a bad memory with no proof those years ever happened. This let me reconstruct you the way I wanted to remember you. I felt vindictive—I could shape you into what I wanted you to be, what I wanted you to have been. It was like I had my revenge at last.

I wrote about how scarred I was by our friendship; in the first version, however, I had to lie, writing a tidy end where you showed up in my backyard, screaming that you were my best friend, followed by an unexplainable, immediate admission to a drug treatment center. I pretended you never contacted me again. I pretended you called yourself my best friend. I titled the piece "Ties That Bind," epigraphed it with those haunted last two lines from the chorus of "Carolina in My Mind," published it in my university lit journal as nonfiction, and that was satisfying, for a while, though it troubled me on the reread to see that I had called myself Bañana, your nickname.

I decided to adopt a pill addiction, because I wanted to know what it felt like to be addicted. I selected caffeine pills because they seemed the least obtrusive and the easiest to obtain. I sought out Vivarin in the Osco Drug aisles because I remembered your yellow pills, but they were unavailable so I bought an off-brand. I had a measured approach: I planned to take one-half of a pill on the first day, a whole pill on the second day, and increase by halves until I was taking a bottle every day. But after the second day, I didn't feel myself craving the caffeine. I barely noticed the effects. I was not high. I was not jittery. So I abandoned my "addiction" before it even began.

I smoked pot for the first time that same year in college, one hour after I drank alcohol for the first time. I thought of you as I sloppily inhaled, as I turned my grimace into a smile while I sipped, wondering what you would say if you saw me. I thought of how you never offered to show me, to share with me, like you'd decided I wasn't cool enough.

I wasn't a snitch. You have to believe me. I never snitched on you. I kept your secrets from my parents; I lied to your mom and said you were taking a shower the morning after you'd not slept over, instead staying out in Bath with Hannah and doing some "shit." I lied to anyone who asked about you. I protected your secrets like a guard dog, humbling myself, hiding myself, trying to prove my loyalty. I twisted your mean words on the answering machine and told my concerned parents they were an inside joke. I defended your need to be dropped off at Pizza Inn to meet up with someone who had some shit—just, MOM, it's fine, she knows someone who will give her a ride home, why can't you just drop her off?—allowing myself to bear the brunt of the questioning. I protected your lies because I loved you.

My attempts to control our story alarmed me; my attempts to reframe our story confused me. I tried to analyze female adolescent friendships for my senior honors thesis, editing out the false conclusion of my "nonfiction" piece and admitting, instead, that what I feared most was the inevitable phone call that would come. I feared that you would find me before I could find you. What puzzled me was how I knew I would want to pick up the phone and prove I had always been your friend, even when you couldn't see it. But I ended up dropping the project entirely, leaving behind a cluster of half-rewritten documents with titles like "Ties with Less Lies," recognizing, even then, that there were fictions I still needed to believe.

That's when you call me again. I am home in Indiana visiting my parents for a long weekend, which is an abnormal occurrence, so it does and does not surprise me when I answer the house phone and a flat, dry, spit-the-words-out voice asks, "Do you know who this is?" Of course I don't, but as my stomach clenches when you say your name, of course I do. You tell me you're waterskiing in a town forty minutes away with your parents and your son. You don't stutter. Your son. He's three years old and mean and sarcastic—wonder where he got that from, right? You have a husband in the Marines you married right out of high school, but you didn't take his last name. You couldn't really see yourself as a Hernandez, haha. You're living in North Carolina again, can I believe it?

I have walked like a zombie into the front yard and time has decelerated. It is warm and humid and I am hiding my phone call from my mother as you monologue at me. It occurs to me that I should be taking notes, so I dash back into the house to grab a piece of paper and a pen. This is fodder, after all, which is what makes me interrupt you and ask what made you stop doing drugs, amazed at my own forthrightness, knowing the worst you can do is hang up. You say, "Well, it's kind of hard to do that stuff when you're a Christian," and I wait for your derisive laugh, indicating that was a joke, but it never comes. That might surprise me more than your child, your husband, your presence in my state, your prescience at knowing I was home in a home where I no longer lived.

You have to go, so you ask for my phone number at college. I hedge, horrified, and say we haven't really gotten the phone line set up yet; I don't know what the phone number is. The absurdity of the lie strikes me and quickly, so I don't seem rude, I ask for yours instead, promising to call you sometime, knowing I will never call you. I have been immersed in the metaknowledge of "Cat's Eye" and I know that, like Elaine, when importuned by Cordelia to save her, I should also refuse. But I write your phone number on the edge of my notes anyway.

When I reenter the house, I must look stunned because my mother asks who it was. When I say your name, she rises from the couch to enfold me in a hug I cannot accept because it humiliates me too much; to see my mother's reaction clarifies that she knows, she knew. I need to be alone, I need to focus on my pain, conserve my strength, ignoring your outstretched arm, fool-me-once-shame-on-you-fool-me-twice-shame-on-me, snubbing the humbleness it took to call me when I'd never returned your call seven years earlier. It is a bitterness I believe I have earned on the thin trail of selfishness that *I walk along.*

——

I am standing still. And yet I walk head down, into the unmoving wind, the details of your life surrounding me as I enter the eye of the hurricane.

I hunt you down methodically, doggedly, for years. I google your name, I google your child's name, and then I google Marine bases in North Carolina. I find your name on a list of bachelor's degree recipients in 2004, earning your degree summa cum laude—in four years! With a four-year-old child! In special education—SPECIAL EDUCATION! After your cupped shoulder slaps in eighth grade! And I find your name on a list of MBA recipients three years later, in a new town at a new university, still in North Carolina. It surprises me to see your committed return to the state I thought had rejected us both. I google myself and try to gauge the access: Can you know where I live? How to contact me? I believe you will.

I find your second marriage announcement, though I never find your divorce judgment from the first. I find your husband's office and I find the town where you are living, which is beside the suburb where my best friend from high school lives. I think about the times I flew to visit her, how you were just down the road, how I didn't even know.

I find your Facebook profile, I find your name on a swing dancing website, I find your name on a website devoted to a specific dog breed. I find your parents, I find your married sister. And then, one day, I find your obituary.

It is an afternoon like most other fall afternoons: I am avoiding work by googling people I once knew because autumn has always swept in with a cold undercurrent of nostalgia. I can tell the year is ending when I start longing for the people I have lost. I type in your name—your new married name because while you did not take Hernandez when you married your first husband (but were you ever married? I cannot confirm this beyond your mention in the last phone call that Gretchen was the maid of honor in your first wedding), you did change your last name with your second marriage. A link comes up, previewing the text of your new full name and the words "died July 1, 2011," mentioning your town, "after a brief illness."

I am light headed and my fingers are shaking; I am breathing shallowly as I click the link, certain it is a mistake, certain it is not. When I read your birthdate I know it is correct, but I continue to scan for inaccuracies, disbelieving when I read your parents' names, your siblings' names, and then the brutal, unerring mention of the town we had lived in together.

I am most stunned by "a brief illness" as the cause of your death, and I continue to google your name for the rest of the afternoon in a cold sweat, but I find no further details. Do I deserve to know? How can I deserve to know anything about your life when you offered it to me, once more, seven years earlier and I rejected your advances? How can I deserve to know anything about your death?

You are survived by your two sons, but there is oddly no mention of your second husband in your obituary, though he survives you as well—I know this because in the years to follow, I hunt him down, trying to find proof he remarried, wondering what he did with two sons, one biological and one adopted. Did your older son stay with your second husband? Did he move in with his father? Your older son bears your maiden name in the obituary, so I guess neither of you was a Hernandez after all.

It is disbelief, it is relief. It is a coda where I expected a repeat bar, a locked door when I thought it was only closed. I can't bring myself to tell my husband what I have discovered until we are in bed and the lights are out; I can't bear my face to be seen as I sob out the scant facts, grimacing my lips so wide in a scream-cry they almost look like a smile. Your death has made my refusal to forgive into a crime, rather than a reluctant accession I planned to make when the time was right, when I'd had my moment of maturation. And I forgive you so wholly, so instantly upon learning of your death that it frightens me, because the alternative, holding a grudge against someone who can never do me wrong again, is disgusting, a violation.

I am afraid of the petulant, foot-stamping twelve-year-old, screaming that it's not FAIR that you left; I still NEED you. I need you so I can hate you. I need you so I can forgive you. *There are days when I can hardly make it out of bed.*

———

You're dead, Cordelia. No I'm not. Yes you are. You're dead. Lie down.

But in my dream, you were still alive. We were in a room, in a house, at a sleepover. We were vaguely the age I am now—we weren't twelve again—but the specifics didn't matter because we were adults. I was uneasy until I remembered, "She's supposed to be dead. But she's here now, so she CAN'T be dead. That means she's still alive," and I was relieved the door hadn't slammed shut; there was still time to reconcile.

I dream you alive more than I dreamed of you when you were alive. Your vanishing and reappearing acts left me mistrusting finality. You came back when you weren't supposed to come back; you came back when I had invoked you. If I believe you are dead, you cannot come back, and I want you to come back. Yet I want you to stay put. I want to believe I want you to come back so I can be someone other than who I am: the girl who could not forgive or forget. I do not want you to come back because I do not want to be the girl I am: the girl still craving one last acknowledgment that you are sorry, like this time it will be enough.

Cordelia returned three times. I believed that by the third I would be ready to rinse off the pain, retaining the marrowed truth that for those first two preadolescent years in North Carolina, we made a box to keep out the people who told us we didn't belong. I didn't have to construct it alone; you gave me the blueprints, you held up the supports. How can I beg you to return, again, so I can reject you, again?

I think of your neighbor trying to court you, using a nickname that was meant to endear her to you by recalling something familiar. She didn't know you'd shed that identity, that it was inevitable you'd slough her off as well, leave her peering out from behind the curtain, watching as we regressed and made ourselves sad to "Sesame Street" music, cementing our vulnerabilities by exposing our childhoods. How couldn't I have seen I would lose you too? You waffled between wanting to be a child and wanting to be a teen and when you decided to make your final break for it, I was left behind.

We were confused, together, and then we were confused together, two Hoosiers claiming kinship somewhere so foreign to North Carolinians that half my eighth-grade yearbook signatures wished me luck in India. So we mocked their accents and we mocked their traditions of naming their daughters after their mothers, and I slept on the trundle bed your mom had hopefully purchased, and we walked our collies together, as twin-like as we could be.

I loved you like I'd never loved a friend before because I'd never needed a friend so badly before. I'd never been so grateful to have someone willing to teach me how to shave my forearms so the hairs wouldn't appear so dark. I couldn't know they would sun-bleach as I aged, tiny fuzz worn down by time. I couldn't know you wouldn't be around to see that I'd grown. How can you possibly have died at twenty-nine; what illness could have felled you? How brief is "brief"?

I feel July approaching, but your life was always synonymous with death, your birthday too close to Kurt Cobain's suicide, premature conclusions for you both, inextricably linked for me. What else can I write? I don't have the right. You were married. You are buried. You're lying in a grave, and *I'm lying on the floor.*

———

**It's old light, and there's not much of it. But it's enough to
see by**, enough to see you walking past me in your Banana
Republic logo T-shirt, arms crossed, dissatisfied. It's enough
to see myself, pain bright in my eyes, beside an unclaimed bus
seat I won't let anyone else sit in, waiting for you to change
your mind. It's enough to see us stuffing notes into each other's lockers, leaving messages on answering machines, recognizing "All Apologies" on the radio and quickly turning it off,
or turning it up.

To say I miss you is reductive. How can I miss you when
I see you everywhere, unwillingly, hungrily? How can I hate
you when you gave me the conclusion I claimed I longed for,
an end to our story, no revelations left to dread?

Your obituary has been archived, the memory book de-
activated. I keep the dead link to my discovery bookmarked
on my computer to remind myself that it really happened,
but the years get slipperier and truth is overlaid with a fiction. I'm locked in the narrative "Cat's Eye" provides, only
able to brace myself through a reread every couple of years,
surprised each time I find another similarity, another coping
mechanism I internalized, another detail I'd thought came
from my life, not Elaine's. I collect the first and last lines of
each section in bolds and italics, reordering them in a cat's eye
where the end collides with the beginning; the denouement
is the rising action. By bending the story, it's like watching
the adult Elaine spread her arms and jump from the bridge
only to find herself standing on the bridge again as a child,

a Sisyphean paralysis, unable to grow up, unable to regress, restlessly trapped inside a marble.

I ended my first piece about you traumatized by a closure that never happened; I ended the second desiring a phone call that you accommodated. Margaret Atwood ended hers missing something that could never happen, so I dream of you still, waiting for my phone to ring. You are dead, but you have come back from the place you were supposed to stay before. When I hear Kurt Cobain's voice, disembodied, plaintively insisting that he will take all the blame, my head lightens; it is a portal to an emptiness that twisted and turned back on me, not my fault, my fault. *Time is not a line but a dimension.*

Out Line

Project description:
A return to an in-between place, a liminal place, a preadolescent place with four years of phantom occupation. The town never admitted I was there, but a dash between 1992 and 1996 doesn't make this an epitaph. History needs beginnings and ends, but not my history.

An outline, a delineation of the line that I traced out, or the one encircling the city that kept me out.

It is a trip I have taken for years; the errata litters my Google search history. I sent the historical society fifty dollars for the thirteen-hundred-page county chronicles so I could learn the secrets of every family profiled. But the families submitted their own stories, I realized partway through, so now I am paying attention to what is included, and what is absent.

Pitt County has always been over one-third Black. But the family histories in the book are nearly all white.

My middle school bore the name of C.M. Eppes, a reference to the principal of the Black high school which had mysteriously burned down in 1970. Its destruction had forced the county's hand, and the long-delayed desegregation finally occurred as the Black students joined the white students at Rose High School on Elm Street. Twenty years later, the conjoined student body moved to a newly built high school, and the former Rose was converted into a middle school—C.M. Eppes Middle—one year before I began sixth grade.

The soapstone lab tables had decades of gum adhered to the undersides, a constellation of colors. It was not all spearmint white.

I will return to that town, hog-belly-up on the coastal plains of North Carolina, to document what I wanted to see but did not. Or I will document what I did not want to see but did. I will produce an essay about the essay I will write about the essay I would write if I had to actually return.

Here is my cable cord, here is my fractal wire, here is my spider thread. All I have to do is open a browser.

Product of the funded activity:
The disorientation I already know. Things have changed, things have not. Arrival was like a choked inhale, departure like a choked exhale. I will take out my yearbook and look up everyone on the Pitt County tax assessor website so I can drive by their adult houses. Maybe I will catch a glimpse of someone, like the time in 2005 when I saw the thin Mr. Grayson, which will make me reconsider the futures I assumed were fixed.

I will leave out the nice encounters, or I will reframe them with the skepticism of a girl who remembers the sight of her broken diary in a friend's hands, a mother looming behind, when the doorbell rang.

I will circle my old house like the boys who had loitered on my shadowed porch, a Friday midafternoon when everyone was in school. They never dreamed there was a feverish girl peering through the blinds. I called the police because I was thirteen and home sick and alone and I was scared because the boys left my porch but didn't leave. In my driveway, one boy had picked up a metal pole by the basketball hoop, feinted like he was going to hit my dog. When the police arrived, the boys scattered into the ditch creek behind my house. After rustling the boys up by the scruff of their shirt necks and tossing them into the back of the car, the police told me they'd asked the boys what they were doing in this neighborhood because they obviously didn't belong there.

I should have mentioned the boys were Black. I should have mentioned that when Bojangles started building on the corner lot, someone spray-painted *get your black restaurant out of our white neighborhood* on the brick wall. I should have mentioned that the neighborhood kids biked over for Bo-Berry Biscuits anyway. I should have mentioned the boys were my age, and that both white and Black boys my age had gotten OSS—Out of School Suspension, not ISS—at my middle school for bringing guns.

The window has been open while I've been elsewhere. I will lick the yellow pollen that's settled on my shoulder; I will spit and rub a circle on the windshield until I can see where I'm parked.

Activities/Process/Methodology:
Will I drive or will I fly? Won't I want my mix tapes—tapes, not iTunes playlists—in the car with me? Will I want to hear Toni Braxton, Janet, SWV? I'll need to rebuy them if I do. Maybe I'll go to the mall with the cemented graveyard in the middle of the parking lot. If I am unable to locate a music store, I will flip the top of my notebook and scribble *sic transit gloria mundi.*

I will wait to hear the right songs on the radio. Or I won't. They are there, somewhere; I am there and those are the familiar chords of "Carolina in My Mind." But I cued them up.

I have chosen my Airbnb, a house barely a block away from the house where I lived. I've picked my weekend—the hundredth anniversary of the county fair, the last weekend of September. I will buy a soft pack of Marlboros from the vending machine on the east side of the Holiday Inn up the road from Annie's house, shoving in quarters the way she did, and I will pay attention to how my body reacts to the old smell of tobacco smoke. Maybe I'll inhale for the first time in my life as a performative metaphor for how living there damaged me.

I will dissect the neighborhood names of "Westhaven" and "Club Pines," the conjoined places that made up my world, to emphasize how it was both a haven for white people in the southwest of the city and a club bordered by tall pines like a fence.

My daughters cannot come. My husband cannot come. My parents and my siblings cannot come. The only person I want to retread those years with me is dead, which is why she is the only one I want.

I will see if I can drive, by memory, the route Sherman took as he bused us from Club Pines into our school in the decaying pit of the city. Past the Piggly Wiggly, past the mortuary catty-corner from my elementary. I don't remember the mortuary being there when I was a student, but the reference is too elegant to leave out. The Google Maps car captured a man on the front porch of one of the shotgun houses that faced the fifth-grade wing of my school; I will recount the time my teacher had to call the cops because the rap was blasting so loud we couldn't hear her trying to instruct us. They've removed the barbed wire from the top of the chain-link fence that surrounded the playground, but now I'm not sure if the barbed wire was really ever there or if we just wanted it to be.

I will get a guest pass to tour Eppes, find the USS trapdoor in the band room we always swore was where the really bad kids got Under School Suspension. It'll be football season. I can smell the pigs roasting in the massive grills under the stadium rows down the street at Ficklen.

I know how I need to look. I'm growing my hair out, I'm practicing my foundation. I'll buy an old T-shirt at Goodwill, a company with a regional name that can't be found everywhere, but I won't wear the shirt until I'm on my way back home. Then I'll write about how I wear that town on me like a brand.

I have returned a hundred times; I have never come home.

Budget justification:
The Airbnb is ridiculously cheap—something like $59/night
for the entire house. The listing shows three bedrooms, two
of which have unframed beds on the floor. The new owner is
only half trying. That neighborhood used to mean something.
I will work the word "crestfallen" into the essay somewhere
to echo Crestline Boulevard, the street with my house. The
Airbnb is only thirty numbers down from mine. The Airbnb
is actually my brother's friend's old house—I confirmed that
through the county tax assessor website because I wasn't sure
I had remembered correctly.

But the backyard is the reason I want that house—I want
access to the ditches snaking through the neighborhood. I
will live out my fantasy of rafting through the drainage. I
have mapped their paths. I know I can enter the ditch behind
the Airbnb and paddle until I am behind my own house. It is
the only way I can get into my old backyard, now, because
the new owners put up a six-foot fence surrounding what we
used to leave wide open.

The people to whom my parents sold our house twenty-
three years ago are the people who still own it. Their daughters are married, their son has left town, the old man is near
retirement age. I have to go to my house before they leave,
while my last name might still carry currency. I will stand
on the front porch and prove I lived there once; I will ask if
they still have the hook-and-eye latches on the cubby doors
leading under the eaves in the upstairs bedrooms. I will ask if
they ever found the shark teeth we strained from the creek
and brought back in our pockets, little bite-threats, still sharp
thousands of years later.

I will promise, like the Miranda Lambert song, that if they will just let me in I won't take anything from the house that broke me.

Nowhere hurts like the place you learned to be hurt; nowhere hurts like the place you were a preadolescent. I will not think of the empty stairwell where I stopped to remove the sports bra I did not need, wiping at my underwear with jean pocket corners that I inspected, looking for red and never finding it. I will not think of the bus seat with the hand thrust over the top, his quick fury when I declined to draw a star on him because he was a boy, not because his skin was darker, shame that I could not vent because I was afraid of men. The answering machine messages filled up the tape, playback I would muffle with my thumb.

I will go to the site of the old Pier One and tuck dollar bills onto any shelf to pay off the change purse I stole. I will go to Brody's and buy any prom dress I want because I cannot have the jean vest and white tulle skirt I desired when I was thirteen. I will buy myself a lot of things as reparations, and when I get home, I will lay them out on my bed, photograph the lot, and store it all away in a box I will not open because I just need to possess. It will be an adroit metaphor for the entire trip.

Project timeline:
Can I bring myself to eat at Ragazzi's? Will I allow myself to be buttered up with breadsticks? Will I go to the head shop and buy the butterfly polymer clay candle holder out of spite? Do I even still want it?

I will contemplate moving my family there, that much I know. I will tell myself that if I can just get a membership to the Lake Ellsworth pool, my daughters' adolescence would be different. They don't have to be northerners coming in clueless. I can give them cotillion, teach them how to slur *-ville* into *-vul*.

I will not remember to check my privilege because when I lived there, I thought I had none. But in that town, every white person does.

I'm in the county fair building with the pumpkin I entered in the decorating contest, the white one I painted with splotches of brown, hooked with sunglasses, and angled a floppy black hat atop, an honorable mention ribbon tagged on my Michael Jackson. I didn't have to get an honorable mention; not every contestant did. I will compare that memory to the Gravitron, the feeling of being pinned against the wall as the floor dropped out, stuck in whatever position I had assumed, arms either indefensibly splayed open or else crunched against my chest, my own weight crushing myself.

I will reference the apocryphal line I said when my family first moved there, the one where I swore *I cried when we arrived but I'll laugh when we leave.* I will not mention that I cried when we did actually leave, or else I will make a reference to a familiar syndrome, ham-handedly renaming it Stokes-home for the county town nearby.

Of course I will cry when I leave because all leavings are like the first one.

When I get back to the Midwest, I will note the humidity, how it's different. How the prairie sun burns but doesn't leave the same slick sweat coat on my skin, a damp sunscreen I always tried to wipe off. I could not recognize the secrets that place tried to reveal to me, which is why I have to return over and over until I learn that I don't have to return. I will always witness what I want.

Contribution to the field/conceptual importance:
There will be something I have forgotten that I will disclose at the end. I said "disclose," but I wrote "enclose" the first time. I'm still watching for the out line.

The wallpaper in the bathroom of the Airbnb house reminds me of the wallpaper in my old bathroom, which is another reason I will rent that house. I will comb through the rooms at leisure, finding the right place to perform the displacement game. If I curl on the floor facing the same direction I once faced, covering my exposed arms with my childhood blanket, I can transpose locations—as long as I keep my eyes closed, I am actually there, in my old house. All the physical facts are in place.

I have had dreams where I rented my old house, but there were rooms that didn't exist. These are the portals I will access to slip through memory into the places I didn't want to see when they were corporeal.

It will all seem smaller, closer. It always does.

The tobacco fields that have turned into an extension of the subdivision will be representative of the town building atop its history. I will not use those houses as emblems of progress, because progress means growth and too many things have remained the same.

A few years after I left, the parents' association filed a lawsuit against the public school board, alleging that their white kids were being discriminated against: they were still being forced to desegregate lower-income elementary schools nearly fifty years after *Brown v. Board.* The town moved with its own deliberate speed, building an elementary school near my old neighborhood that the board claimed the burgeoning southside population required. Then the town tucked under its lower lip, sliding a court-approved policy across the table: *race cannot be the sole measure of diversity.*

There used to be a house I remembered on the way out to the new hospital, which is no longer new. The house had a wide circle driveway; the house was set back far from the road. The house was two stories tall with white pillars and it looked like Tara in *Gone with the Wind.* If the house is no longer there, I will describe the old South making way for the new. Or constructions of the South being replaced with new construction. If it stands, I will find some way to tear it down.

In the Burn Pile Behind the Old Nobles House

Plastic Meeko glass, a Pocahontas Burger King promo
We entered through the kitchen, a grime-coated galley with crust-chunked plates stacked in the sink and flaking white cupboards with half-hanging doors and a Formica table squeezed against the wall, and I curled up my toes in my sandals, involuntarily. The effluvia of decades in the house, the damp, hanging gloom of humidity because there was no central air conditioning and the painted-over windows couldn't open. Down the hall was a small faded-paper bedroom, and crammed between the dresser tops heaped with Looney Tunes beefy tees was the bed. That was where her mother and Trey lived. There was a deadbolt on their bedroom door, the front door was uselessly skeleton-keyholed, and the back screen door was flapping, the hook-and-eye unlatched.

Three-inch-thick phone book
Two years earlier, I had been befriended by a girl who also lived in Club Pines. When her mother remarried, the girl

received a stepsister whose cleverness and willingness to engage in make-believe worlds drew me to her. I ignored the original girl and only came over on weekends to see her stepsister. She and I invented sister cities named Tylacia and Lovers Lane, populating them with the families we fantasized about: Tazz and Scarlett Claiborne, a movie producer and his stay-at-home wife; Kevin and Mona Farice, a paramedic and Tylacia's first female mayor; Jennilyn Janswood, the new fourth-grade teacher. We assigned our citizens pen pals in their neighboring towns, and we would perch on the slipper chairs in the front sitting room of her stepmother's house, scribbling their get-to-know-you letters, throwing the folded papers across the carpet to each other, waiting for someone to write back.

Videocassette in a padded manila envelope

We were new builds, my friend and I. My parents had upgraded from a flat ranch in Oregon to the two-story splendor of eastern North Carolina, and her parents had come south from New York, though they separated shortly afterward. Her mother was now living in an old white clapboard out near Ayden with Trey, the son of the family who owned the fields behind my neighborhood. My friend lived with her mother during the week. As she neared the end of eighth grade, my friend became fixated on attending boarding school. She sent away for promotional materials and I followed suit, confusing my parents as I received mailed videocassettes from the Madeira School, girls rappelling through forests in their green plaid skirts, gorgeous ivy-covered brick buildings revealing classrooms of students earnestly discussing science and math in their dormitories and dining halls. I felt I needed to purchase a history for my descendants if we were ever going to belong in the South, but I didn't want to actually leave my family behind. I wanted the labyrinth of ancestry, but I would settle for the clutched fist of ownership obtained through nine-tenths of the law.

Matted green shag carpet

Across from her mother and Trey's bedroom was a living room, dark and murky because I don't think there was an overhanging light fixture. The windows looked out at the shin-brushing weeds of the front yard, but the blinds stayed pulled; too much light would heat up the room too quickly. A room air conditioner made it tolerable. A long, worn couch, an old television, and more furniture and boxes girding the perimeter. I slept somewhere in that room, once, and I assume my friend slept on the couch because it was where she slept five times a week, but I fuzzed that night from my memory.

Roach husks

Up the stairs were the two bedrooms no one lived in anymore. The roof needed patching, and after a good rain, streams would drip-drop into the bedrooms my friend and her brother had abandoned, though their stuff was still spread everywhere. Clothes my friend had outgrown, old school projects, and the ephemera of life that she left in place, didn't pack out in her weekend knapsack but also didn't throw away. There was a large, lawyer-looking desk that I was instantly drawn toward. It had a broad leatherette ink-blotter tabletop and a cunning, thin brass fence standing along the back of the desk. I admired the desk loudly, and my friend said I could just have it. Trey and her mother muscled the desk down the stairs, banging into the walls, and heaved it into Trey's truck bed, where my friend and I held the legs in place as they drove me back to Club Pines, the wind greasing my hair.

Elsa Peretti for Halston, bean-shaped locket with solid perfume wax

My friend's mother and Trey had found ten $100 bills, dated to the 1920s, buried inside the wall of their bedroom—a stash they assumed was from Depression days, when the Nobles had owned the house. It was never clear how or why they went hammering in the walls, but their discovery convinced my friend and me that there was money squirreled away in other places. We had elaborate plans to jackhammer the stairs apart once her mother bought the double-wide she was angling to slide into the tired-out tobacco fields alongside the house. We were going to demo the place like the Bobbsey Twins, surely finding a secret not meant for us to discover.

Moon pie wrappers

We did not go to boarding school; we did not carry out our plans to marry my cousin and his friend in Alabama, where it was legal if you were thirteen. Wednesday Utah wrote a letter to Jennilyn Janswood, informing her that Lovers Lane had burned to the ground, leaving my Tylacians stranded. My friend's mother and Trey moved into the mobile home and it was clean and fresh, a 1995 model with a vaulted ceiling and beige carpeting, well lit, nothing like the dark, cluttered, wet history I'd wanted to burrow into. I could find aspiration anywhere. What I couldn't find was the collapsed core of a home, broken into parts I could steal.

A Pit Is Removed, a Hollow Remains: *Chronicles of Pitt County*, Revisited

Excavation Report

Nontechnical summary

I have been modifying history for decades. I have been claiming it and recasting it and inserting myself while dipping the documents in tea, crumpling them up and letting them dry before spreading them out on the table as evidence. When I was a child, I took the peso I'd received in a fast food meal and I paired it with the yen I'd been mailed by a school-issued pen pal, and I forged a treasure map for my siblings, leading them to the banks of the drainage ditch that I'd salted with a currency only useful elsewhere. I was trying to give them something I wanted. I wanted to believe there was a map. I wanted to believe I could uncover something hidden.

Introductory statement

I moved to Pitt County, North Carolina, in 1992. I moved away from Pitt County, North Carolina, in 1996. That four-year span also constituted my early adolescence. I spent the following twenty-two years spying on the county online, imagining myself back into the county, revisiting the county, rewriting myself into the county. In 2018, I stumbled upon the *Chronicles of Pitt County*, an 876-page collection of history self-published by the Pitt County Historical Society in 1982, coincidentally the same year I was born. The first 150 pages of the book are dedicated to the first three hundred years of Pitt County's history, from its origination in the King of England's 1663 land grant all the way through desegregation in the 1960s. The meat of the book consists of the self-submitted family histories from the people of Pitt County during the early 1980s. If the residents could write their own versions of their histories and then have them codified into truth, couldn't I do the same? Couldn't I finally force my history into the place I most wanted to belong?

So I took the book. I took the book apart. I grafted my history onto theirs; I twisted the lessons until I could wring out similarities between my past and theirs; I removed and imprinted my history on top of theirs until I could not tell the difference between their truth and mine.

Geological/topographical background

I kept archives. I had digital archives, bookmarked websites I moved from computer to computer over the years, and I also had physical archives, talismanic objects I retained through my moves as proof to myself that those events had really happened. I taught myself to track the local Pitt County newspaper through their website on reflector.com, clicking Vital Stats every couple of weeks to see who was engaged, married, or part of a wedding party. I did not look at the burials, though I should have. I arrowed through Google Maps on Street View; I narrowed to my neighborhood on Airbnb and broke into houses, wandering through rooms I'd been in and houses I'd biked past. I entered addresses in the Pitt County Tax Assessor website and confirmed contracts, confirming residences for parents who still own the houses I remember their children in. I have not physically been to Pitt County in fifteen years. It doesn't matter. I have been there fifteen hundred times in my mind.

Historical background

My parents were born and raised in northern Minnesota, surrounded by their extended family. My parents left northern Minnesota before I was born. I visited northern Minnesota less than five times before I left for college. Those facts are all true. Three more true sentences: my parents referred to northern Minnesota as "home" for twenty-seven years before they moved back. I called four different states home before I made my own. Displacement was my core fear and my core reality.

The reality is that I did not miss home until I realized others had one.

I grew up in pioneer country, the heart of the Oregonian valley Lewis and Clark had sought, where white history was as young as Frederick Jackson Turner's frontier thesis. I moved backward with my family, reversing the trail, slinking across the country and sinking into the megalodon-riddled creeks of Pitt County, North Carolina, teeth sunk millions of years ago but erupting from the creek beds in a new row every spring, endless proof of inhabitation.

The land did not need me. The people did not need me. I had no gray rag wrapped around a sword hilt, no hoop-skirted bellwethers painted in portraits around the parlor. I didn't know what fresh tobacco smelled like until the week I arrived, the sweet heaviness cloying the air down by the Health, Physical Education, Recreation and Dance university building where my father would work. The old tobacco warehouse was still in use then, though it is gone now, replaced by a Dollar General. I can't find hard evidence the warehouse was actually there, but I know it was.

General and specific aims of fieldwork

As a child, I owned an orange hardback book of basic archaeology, and I had annotated the book with my best green calligraphy pen, asking questions like "What does Trois-Frères mean?" beside the cave paintings or "Druids?" next to the famous line drawing of Stonehenge. I saw these early notes as part of my archive, the earliest inclinations of my fixation with cracking open the rib cage of fact. I was going to find truths, hidden in the codification of history, and release their booby traps, nimbly stepping out of the way before injury. I was willing to manufacture the traps.

I came to the *Chronicles of Pitt County* for access, for secrets, a mouse in a crumbledown tunnel sneaking away with my morsels of information. I did not want to understand as much as I wanted to possess. If I held the county's history, I could hold its future, and I could wiggle my way in between the cracks. I wanted to find the cracks so I could stick a crowbar inside and break them open. Histories are recorded by the victors; histories are remembered by the losers.

Methodology

I envied the children with names derived from the county heirs. I scrabbled down gullies, I straddled the split-rail fence around the tobacco field behind the neighborhood playground, lifting the furrow scrap cast aside after the planting, watching the clods explode into powder when I hurled them against the fence posts. There was no evidence I had been there. No one knew what I had done. No one knew I had briefly possessed the leavings no one cared for, no one noticed anymore.

Results

See: enclosed.

Biases

I am white, and so I fixated on what white girls in my neighborhood appeared to have—access, acceptance, wealth, security. My parents had only been able to class-ascend into Club Pines because our old house in Oregon had doubled in value. I still wore Keds-knockoffs to gym class and bought my clothes at Goodwill because I couldn't bring myself to ask for a sweater at Brody's. I remembered how tight times had been. I had not grown up with racial disparity or segregation before moving to Pitt County—there hadn't been much diversity where I had lived before—so I saw class striation as financial, period.

In Pitt County, I watched white mothers lock the car doors when a Black man was walking the crosswalk in front of their car. I heard classmates say words I'd only read with asterisks. They didn't even flinch or drop their voices. I have spent over twenty-four years unlearning behaviors I only witnessed for four years; I have spent years cringing as the implications of my inactions become clear. The history of Pitt County is a part of my history.

I wonder if the families in the *Chronicles of Pitt County* feel exposed. I assume they didn't predict someone outside the county would be reading the book, much less sharing their stories. They could not have predicted me.

Discussion/Conclusion

It is important to understand that the *Chronicles of Pitt County* is self-published by the Pitt County Historical Society. This book's veracity was not vetted in a fact-checking branch of a publishing house; no one teaches this book in school. Yet it's the closest thing to an official document the county has. These family histories are all self-submitted hand-me-downs recorded into the annals. I think about who selected in. The number of Black histories included in this book would barely fit under a fingernail in this fistful of town scions. The families secure in their importance, the Minges (of East Carolina University's Minges Coliseum) and the Sheppards (of the Sheppard Memorial Library), didn't seem to feel the need to participate. But then they had nothing to confirm, no need for a land grant deed matted and framed in their entry halls. Their histories are known by the ones who matter.

Support data

Pitt County took pride in being the home of Henry Lawson
Wyatt, the first Confederate soldier to die in battle during
the Civil War. But on the 150th anniversary of Wyatt's death
in 2011, a North Carolina Archives historian debunked that
myth, granting the first casualty to a Virginian who was killed
nine days before Wyatt, pointing out that, anyway, Wyatt
was actually born in Virginia—Wyatt only moved to Pitt
County as an adolescent. Wyatt's statue and its historically
inaccurate plaque remained in front of the North Carolina
State Capitol building, unchanged until its removal—along
with many other Confederate monuments throughout the
South—during the summer of 2020.

Figures

Club Pines and Westhaven neighborhoods, 1992–1996

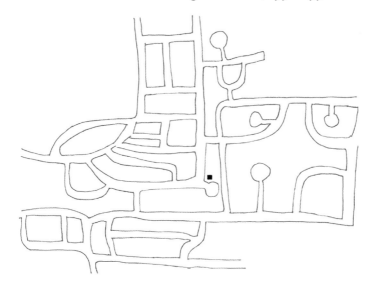

References

Pitt County Historical Society, Inc. *Chronicles of Pitt County, North Carolina*. Hunter Publishing Company, 1982.

Taylor, James. "Carolina in My Mind." *Greatest Hits*, 1976.

Grafting

When Abraham was five years old, his grandfather, George, deeded to him a slave boy who on cold winter nights was permitted to sleep at the foot of his feather bed. Exemplifying the attributes of a fine Christian gentleman, [Abraham] was known to be kind to his slaves, some of whose descendants still live today on his land near Schoolhouse Branch (Abraham Darden Moye 534–535).

The importance of close relationships for success in grafting is well known—no one would seriously set out to graft a member of one botanical family with a member of another.

Relationships are descendants are places where facts are sown, weeded, grown. History is a nitrogen deposit, nutrient-leached after three hundred years of planting. When I arrived on the tobacco plains of eastern North Carolina, it was time for crop rotation. I did not realize the fields were only temporarily fallow. I thought there was space to grow, a girl in the grip of a grift.

|

The land that he owns and farms has been in his family for over 220 years. It was purchased by James Crandell from a land grant deed from Lord John Granville, June 26, 1762 (William Alfred Crandell 251).

The proper use of a rootstock lies in the provision of a benevolent foundation for the scion; interaction with particular scions has enabled horticulturalists to gain excellent control of their material.

When my family left the well-documented soil of Oregon's Willamette Valley, I was a whip with my limbs lopped off. Removal from the place I had known as home created a trauma breach, a root desiccation, and I did not transplant well. I considered my new town's official motto, "Find Yourself in Good Company," but I did not realize it was a directive, not an offer.

|

Here they prospered and multiplied so that by 1762, the date of the oldest Pitt County tax list, 12 of the 492 households were headed by Tyson grandsons of Mathias Tyson. Assuming an equal number of Tyson-born wives in other households, one can estimate that even then, 5% of the county residents were the descendants of Mathias Tyson (Mathias Tyson 690).

It has been observed that trees of the same species will form graft-clusters between their roots, symbiotically nourishing each other so thoroughly that if all but one tree in a forest are cut down, the roots of the whole group will still have survived.

I lived in Club Pines on the edge of the suburbs, a southwest diagonal spoke pointing away from the center of the city where my neighbors and I were bused to integrate the public schools. Twelve rows of bus benches divided by an aisle, flute cases and backpacks and backsides squished three to a bench, seventy-two white kids spilling into the school, arms interlocked.

|

Wiley remained at home to help run the plantation, which consisted of 3000 acres of cleared land, 75 slaves, and 75 mules. After the war, he lost everything but lived on a small piece of land the family retained. Wiley was a gentleman and did not know how to work after the war, so Jacob Wilson Higgs had to plow the fields at an early age to help keep them alive (Jacob Wilson Higgs Family 384).

The rootstock merely serves as a nurse until the scion has become connected with the soil; then the rootstock rots away.

It was curing season, the ploughed furrows of tobacco plucked and raftered upside down, flue vents tilted open from beneath, impossible to see between the wooden slats of the shacks, to see the embers stoking a constant, low heat, holdover practices from the old days. Cigarette smoke kills, but as metal fans gently blew air around the drying tobacco, the town was blanketed with a bitter-sweet smell like nostalgia.

|

Orphaned at an early age when yellow fever took all of her family in Selma, Alabama, Mary Elizabeth made the trip to Pitt County on foot with twenty slaves and a wagon full of possessions. Her slaves remained loyal and helped in getting started during the Reconstruction Period (Mary Elizabeth Wordsworth and James Blount Brooks 193).

Land intended for raising rootstocks should be clear of perennial weeds and fallow for at least one year before sowing, during which the land must be thoroughly cleaned.

This is the core: I moved from the cloudy skies of Corvallis, the heart of the valley, to the bright-lit Pitt, the don't-swallow, the can't-chew, the stubborn center. Everything that was once gray was starkly divided into black and white. When a pit is removed, a hollow remains, a curved emptiness shaped around an absence. The pit is usually discarded; its surrounding flesh is the desirable part. But a fruit grows around a pit. What lies inside it is the heart.

|

He was a cousin of General Bradford Forrest, a coura-
geous southern general in the Civil War from Georgia.
General Forrest was bitter with the outcome of the war
and supposedly he was the originator of the notorious
Ku Klux Klan. Ben, as a child, was fascinated with the
fact that his mother, a seamstress, slept in the day time,
and at night she hung bed quilts over the window to
keep the light in so that outsiders could not know that
she was secretively making uniforms for the K.K.K.
(Benjiamen Dixon Forrest Family 314).

The distinguishing feature of approach-grafting is that
those plants to be joined are brought together while each
retains its original parts above and below the point of
contact.

Damaging the fruit is the only way to get to the pit.
Damage is the only way to get to the truth.

|

On many occasions my mother told me of the open air
meat markets. Since she was from the North she had a
pressing fear of a revolt by the blacks (Henry L Rives
Family 598).

The term "incompatible" should not be applied to cases
in which treatment and environment appear to be the
most likely cause of failure.

I wrote letters home to my old friends, explaining the dichotomies of the city and the classroom, how everything was segregated but everyone seemed to prefer it that way. Then I brushed my white-girl hair into a ponytail and got on the bus and blankly stared out the window at the shotgun houses surrounding my barbed-wire-fenced elementary school.

|

In 1899, Bob Turnage, nephew of Theodore L, was murdered by Elijah Joyner, a black man living and working on the farm. While trying to conceal the crime, he burned the store. The last public hanging in Pitt County was that of "Lige" Joyner (Theodore Carlyle Turnage Sr Family 688).

There is no indication that a plant in the mature growth phase will change its compatibility with any given scion as the plant ages.

I didn't know where I lived, but I learned. White girls on one side, Black girls on one side, white girl called a white bitch didn't know why she wasn't just called a bitch. Black boys played on the school basketball team. White boys played Little League, and our town's well-funded team regularly made it to the National Little League World Series. My teachers drawled our state's history: the missing first white child of Roanoke, the Lords Proprietors extending their charter meridians off the map lines all the way to the undiscovered Pacific. But I saw that we were the foot-dragging twelfth colony to sign the Bill of Rights, the second-to-last to secede with the Confederacy. I saw the reluctance to shift positions.

|

The Moye brothers were highly regarded and held in affection by friends of both races. As memorial to this loyal scion of one of America's founding families (1638), his wife and children gave to Pitt County, in 1948, the seventeen and one-half acre site for the Pitt Memorial Hospital (Jesse Rountree Moye Sr 536–537).

A permanent change in one component, brought about by association with another, has never been proved to be other than a temporary influence.

The peach tree I planted, as an adult, caught rotten pit. The peaches grew big and bountiful, sunning their orange faces, and I picked one expectantly, but there was no way I could have known that the core was damaged until I cut into it. The two sides of the peach fell apart in my hands, the pit splitting itself to reveal a pit within the Pitt, the kernel of memory. I threw my spoiled peaches in the compost bin, but their pits remained, littering my potted plants years later after I had finally harvested and spread what I had been allowing to degrade.

|

His land covers a whole school district, with sixty-seven children on his farms. He has a Methodist Church for his colored people, and 250 souls on his farms dependent on his efforts and capital for a living. They occupy thirty-nine residences, well built, and furnished (James E Clark 231).

When a variety becomes obsolete, the grower is reluctant to discard his trees to plant afresh, and that is when he looks with favor on methods of re-grafting.

If I take a seed from an apple and plant it, nurture it, the tree will grow up as a varietal of its parent. A Cortland apple tree does not produce pure Cortland seeds. A sapling grown from a Cortland seed mutates into another iteration, a version of its origin. When I could not claim kin-bones under the farmed-out fields, I felt irrelevant. I slowed my syllables, I swallowed sweet tea, I scraped my knees groveling for invitations, but it all remained on the surface, shallow scratches, a seed parching.

|

A statement that lives with us is—"I'd rather bury you than have you bring an illegitimate child into this world." They gave us values that are priceless. Perhaps my dad was the first black man to own a car in the community mainly because he always wanted ownership and to be somebody (James S and Ellen Brown Jones Family 427).

The root system as well as the branch system may be changed by grafting. The only way to ensure a specific varietal of an apple tree is to snap off a branch and graft that broken limb onto another rootstock.

I got on that bus every day and I stood in line, waiting to enter the assembly, and when the freshly suspended boy turned and threw a lotion bottle at the reinforced glass entrance so hard it cracked, I watched my white vice principal rush outside and tackle the Black boy, holding the boy's arms in a deadlock, frog-marching the boy to the curb and pushing him off school property, and the line kept moving into the gym and I followed and I said nothing.

|

He served on the Greenville City School Board and became the first Black person to ever serve as Chairman in 1977. When Ed was six years old, his father disappeared. There were strong reasons to believe that he was killed by a white man, however nothing was ever done about it and his body was never found (Family of Ed and Jean Carter 223).

Where more than one scion grows from a limb, the better-placed scion must be encouraged by reducing the others until they are eventually entirely removed.

The pit is the seed is the heart is the truth. I was out of place, but I was white in that racially split town. I carried a privilege I did not recognize, and yet I still cried because I was the only girl from Club Pines who didn't attend cotillion.

|

Family stories about the old house include one about unremovable blood stains on the floor, the traces of the murder of the Hanrahans' overseer by a slave (William J and Adelaide Tyson Sermons 614).

Unhealed wounds should be resealed to reduce the danger of the heart-wood rotting.

My father asks me about the time the boys came to our house when I was home alone, the time I crouched in my parents' bedroom and called the police because the boys came to our front door and, after I didn't answer, went around to the side of the house and started walking up the driveway, picking up a long metal pole we used to raise the basketball hoop, menacing at my barking dog. My father asks me what I would have done if I had been on the porch when the boys came up that curving cement path, what I would have said, whether I would have told them to get off our property. I reply that I would have been polite, I would have asked who they were looking for, maybe made a reference to my mom inside if I felt threatened, but I would have been courteous. Concerned that they had the wrong address. My father asks me how I knew something was wrong,

and I reply that I did not recognize the boys. I knew all
the children my age who lived in our neighborhood—
we all rode the bus together—and I did not recognize
those boys. I insist that I was not afraid because the boys
were Black. My father does not ask me whether I would
have called the police if the boys had been white; I do not
revisit that question.

|

In his later years, John's son Louis would remark that he
had heard his father say that if he had fought during the
Civil War, he would have had to fight on the Union side.
Quite a statement from a man whose father had died
at the age of 32 fighting on the Confederate side (John
Wilson Moore and his Descendants 529–530).

Scions must be selected from the parts of the tree which
exhibit the desired characteristics: those should be noted
during the flowering stage.

There was a moment I was both the person I wanted to
be and the person I wanted to believe I would be. And
then there was a reaction, a decision, a gesture, an aver-
sion, a fork when I knew what I felt and how I wanted to
feel, and I dismissed the truth. I cracked into the marrow
of a bone and bound it up in a cast made from the pages
of *Gone with the Wind* and all the right girls signed their
names and drew smiley faces but the cast was eventually
scissored open. The break healed incorrectly, but what

bothered me most was all that evidence of compassion, thrown in the trash.

|

This black pioneer schoolteacher believed that a wholesome knowledge of the past would help his children to more fully appreciate the present as they grew up, and thus stimulate them to strive toward more worthy achievements for the future. All three children felt that their father succeeded in getting this point across to them (William Frank Rich 597).

It is necessary to mention so-called graft-hybrids. This term leads one to suppose that a form of hybridization can be accomplished by grafting, which is not the case. In all probability, no intermingling of characters has ever occurred. What has happened is that two subjects, similar in botanical characters, have joined together at their growing points.

Belonging to a place is not the same as belonging to the place. Recording a history is not the same as recording the history. I belong in eastern North Carolina more now than when I lived there; I know more about its history than I did when I lived there. I reckon with the ways I changed myself and the ways I allowed myself to be changed. I am undoing the past, but there are versions of history grafted to the truth, and there are pits of truth in the wrong soil. Harvest season is over. It is time to see what can be cured.

Piecing

I was born on February 12, 1934, on the farm in Edgecombe County, in the house built by my great-great-great grandfather, Jonas Nelson, Jr. I am directly descended from Jonas Nelson, Jr on both sides of my family. (Archie Vernon and Nannie Louise Bullock Coburn 233)

I was born on July 9, 1982, far from the speck in the caruncle of Lake Superior's great eye which was the house built by my great-grandfather. My grandmother was born in that house; my mother grew up in that house as well. I am directly descended from the Mayflower Pilgrims on both sides of my family, but that ancestry held no weight in Greenville because my forebears had eventually settled in northern Minnesota, not North Carolina.

Most Hardee grandchildren left the farm and one converted to Catholicism in 1968, probably causing those 6 generations of French Huguenots to spin in their graves. The ancestors may have been upset when most descendants moved to professional jobs and left the farm. (David Hardee 356)

My forebears farmed, like many European American forebears—farms in Québec, farms in rural New York, farms in northern Wisconsin. Both of my Lutheran grandfathers converted to Catholicism for their French Canadian and Irish wives. There is an old family farm in rural Wisconsin; I have been there. No one in my family has owned that land for 120 years, but it is still my old family farm. There is also an old family farm in Québec; I have been there too. My great-great-grandfather left that farm to become a voyageur, one of the last, before he immigrated to Wisconsin. Québec holds generations of my family, over 200 years' worth, but those bones have long since decomposed into the soil.

Fourteen of the Rawls are buried in the cemetery in Batesburg. They were so involved in the lumber business that the center marker[s] on the family plots are huge marble stones in the forms of tree trunks. (Rawl-Little Families 593)

My family has been involved in the lumber business for generations. My great-great-grand-father traded farm life in Québec for a farm in Wisconsin smack-dab in the middle of the nine-teenth-century lumber craze. He built a bridge across the Chippewa and the logs slipped beneath; his son, my great-grandfather, followed his fortune to the lumber land of Cloquet, Minnesota, and when the logging was done there too, he worked at the mill, grinding and slicing the logs into toothpicks. My grandfather worked at that mill, my uncles work at that mill, my cousins work at that mill, a logjam legacy.

When I was a young girl, I remember my father using dynamite to blow up tree stumps to clear more needed land and to enable him to purchase more farmland. (Jethro R Mills Family 511)

My great-great-grand-father was out in a back forty, helping a neighbor dig stumps out of the land the lumber barons had left behind, when he had a heart attack three days before Christmas in 1900. My great-grandfather was eight years old when his father died, and every year in his journal, my great-grandfather noted his father's death date and the pain of loss that had never dimmed.

The family farm was located on Nobles Road, "N.C. State Road 1124." Most of the family are buried in the cemetery on the farm that is owned by Speight heirs at this time. (Thomas Nobles Family 566)

I was writing about the house on Pocosin Road where my friend's mother lived, the house where I learned that anyone could purchase a history but it wouldn't necessarily be pretty. My friend's mother was not from the South, but her new husband was. He was the son of the family that owned the fields behind my neighborhood. I did not know that when I began writing about the house on Pocosin Road. I didn't even remember that the house was on Pocosin Road. I had pulled up Google Maps and I followed roads out of town, tracing lines in my memory, looking for the right area. No, that's not true. What I remembered was that there was a grandmother for a neighbor, and the granddaughter was named Kure, and my friend said she was named Kure because her family founded Kure Beach. I googled Kure Beach and then I googled Kure Lane and I found Kure, owning the house her grandmother once owned on Kure Lane, right off Pocosin. It came back to me in a flash, the address, but when I moved down to Street View, nothing was there.

I dragged the cursor to the
west and there it was—the
trailer my friend's mother
and husband had placed
alongside a house that no
longer existed. I wanted
to know who had built
that absent house, so I
dug through the property
records back to the Nobles,
descended from the John
Nobles who had received
Pitt County land in the
1763 land grant. The Nobles
lived all along Pocosin
Road, which intersects
with N.C. State Road 1124;
there is a family ceme-
tery on Pocosin Road.

The house on Pocosin Road
is gone, that ancient and de-
crepit emblem, but I cannot
take my eyes off the ghost
of the Old Nobles House.

Our father, Allen Moye, amazed us as we were growing up because he seemed to know almost everyone in Pitt County and could explain how we were related to many Pitt County families. (Allen Blanie and Pearl Ada Forbes Moye 548)

I wanted to belong to that county harder than I'd ever wanted anything before. Where I had lived before, everyone was new as pioneers and no one sought lineage. In Pitt County, lineage ruled everything. You could claim a kinship by claiming a grave, your DNA sunken and transformed into new soil, the soil that grew new crops that fed the new generation; ancestors had been there for hundreds of years, feeding the same calcium into the teeth that flashed.

When Lu grew up she married a man with ten first names. At the time he was born many friends and relatives wanted to name the new baby. So his parents used all the ten suggestions so that nobody would have hurt feelings. He was named: Arma, Long, George, Mathias, William, John, Adaman, Malivington Corbitt. (Annis Luvenia and George Mathias Corbitt 239)

When I won the crayfish and named it after the three girls whose favor I most wanted, I did not think about the tedium of caring for the crayfish. I didn't know how smelly the river-sweat water inside the fishbowl would get. I didn't think about how you can't play with a crayfish like a puppy. You can't touch a crayfish. And I didn't touch my crayfish; I "released" it into the drainage ditch after a couple of weeks. I was ready to defend my animal activism, but neither Leila nor Annie nor Morgan ever asked after their namesake.

Just prior to the Civil War, William Ashley Manning won $3000 in gold in a lottery. He had to travel to Elizabeth City to collect his prize money, but when he arrived at the Chowan River and learned he had to cross the ferry to get to Edenton, he dreaded the ferry crossing so much that he gave a man $100 to go to Elizabeth City to collect his winnings for him. When the war broke out, he tore up the fireplace hearth in his house and buried the gold, replacing the bricks. It remained in hiding until the war was over and then he dug it up and had this money to help him and his family through the difficult days of reconstruction. (William Ashley Manning 497)

At the house on Pocosin Road, my friend's mother and her husband found ten $100 bills from the 1920s buried in the wall of their bedroom. Seventy-five years had passed since the home had slipped through the fingers of the Nobles, who had owned it when the money was hidden. Perhaps the Nobles could have held onto their property if they'd remembered that ancient thousand dollars they'd saved. I couldn't get over the schadenfreude of knowing the Nobles had lost both their home and their squirreled-away treasure to my friend's mother, a non-native Pitt Countian.

In their home is a prized piece of furniture, known to the family as "the Lafayette chair." (David Lawrence Morrill 533)

I grew up with a beautiful old wooden dresser in our house. The legend was that my parents had bought it at an auction out in the farmlands surrounding Lafayette, Indiana, when my father was a graduate student at Purdue. My parents couldn't have afforded it because they were broke, broke, broke, living in subsidized housing, but they must have afforded it somehow. Quarter-sawn white oak, a mirror that attached on top, three drawers, a relic of the 1920s. I took that dresser with me to college and I have had it ever since. My husband calls it "the Lafayette chest," a moniker it has held since long before I read the *Chronicles of Pitt County*.

John's roots run deep in Pitt County, and after seeing much of the world, he still maintains that this county is the most beautiful place on earth. Instilled in him is a deep love for the land of his ancestors where his great grandfather Whitehurst built his home in 1832. (John Lloyd Watson Sr 708)

I have grown to love land I never lived in, including all the homes my ancestors claimed for me, the places they toiled and disintegrated into, the land where my great-greats built their homes and stayed. But I am also connected to the soil of Pitt County, that temperamental tobacco trace where no matter how many pounds of fresh fertilizer were dumped in, the soil ate it up, the native plants ate it up, consuming anything new and leaving nothing behind once the harvest was over.

Fifty years after she left the farm, Mamie went back to Jolly Old Field with one of her grown sons and sat on the bank of the creek reliving the happy times she had there as a girl. (Mamie Gardner Wooten 746)

I have returned to Greenville three times since I moved away; I have returned to Greenville a hundred times since I left. I have returned with my mother and my sister, I have returned with my best friend, I have returned with my husband. I have driven through the neighborhood where I had only ever biked or walked; I have driven down streets I was only ever driven down. I knew the way to my old middle school by feel after three years of being bused. I knew the way to Lynndale, where my family used to cruise, marveling at the solidity of brick houses where we didn't belong. I went to the river because I remembered where the landing was. I remembered that a person could walk out on the river dock and stand above the milky-brown Tar, but I could not bring myself to reach a hand down into the water. I could not bring myself to touch it. But I didn't need to; it had already pulled me under.

Replacing

The earliest mention of the family is in connection with "Langley Hall" in England and with the heraldic emblem, still used by descendants, with the motto: "J'aimie Jamais." (James Family of Greenville 407)

Joseph Ringgold, my great-grandfather, was a large landowner in Pitt County. His land extended north from Harrington Field along Charles Street to 14th Street, part of Rocky Spring, and Rose High School. Minges Coliseum is on the spot where his home stood. It was torn down when the State took over the land for the University Athletic fields. (Frances Ringgold Smith 617)

Amos liked to watch a bulldozer work. In his swamp land he would watch this machine work hour after hour; for he loved to make more cleared land. Even the land that he inherited from his father, which was mostly woods, and he used mules to clear this land. This land was in virgin pine timber that had never been timbered. (Amos Leon Garris Family 328)

Cedar trees lined the long driveway and a rare, most fragrant grass, yellow Jonquillas, Honeysuckle and Sweet Betsys, the callicanthus shrub, perfumed the air of the whole yard which was enclosed with a snake fence. (Martha Jane Brown Moye 535)

The seasons too were always easily delineated for us during those years of the special cord that kept us tied to Granny's, with the first part of the first season seeming to fall in the late summer. That is when the tobacco markets would open, the streets would be cloudy with yellow dust from the Golden Leaf, and the out of town tobacconists who were staying at Granny's would sit out on the front porch after supper trying to catch a breeze as they spoke of the day's sales. (Matilda Claiborne Moore 522)

Drainage not being what it is today, it was not unusual for the canal which crossed Allen Road just below the Noah Tyson homestead to overflow. At times it would be deep enough that adults and children alike would don bathing suits and go swimming in the road. (Noah Tyson Family 693)

Lena grew up a happy girl, often getting into mischief and many escapades. Her brothers and sisters called her "Skinny" and she almost is to this day. (Raymond Richard McGlohon Family 487)

On frequent trips to New York, Washington, and Richmond she purchased her "ready made" clothes, but kept local gifted seamstresses, of blue-blooded forebears, but living in reduced circumstances due to the aftermath of "The War," busy fashioning dresses and blouses of exquisite handiwork for herself and her children. (Margaret Page Howard Moye 539)

Doris grew up in Grifton where she was affectionately referred to by many who knew her as "the prettiest girl in town." (Doris Mae Brooks Carroll 218/219)

She grew into a beautiful young woman and, while still in high school, was voted "Queen of the Eastern North Carolina Centennial Celebration." At her coronation ball at a Kinston hotel, she enjoyed the festivities but not the dancing because her parents did not approve and she had never learned to dance. (J. Allen Johnston and Mary Alice Smith 423)

Friends were always cordially received in our home, to spend the day, to spend the night, to drop in for meals, or just to visit. Our house parties—lasting two weeks or more, with guests from nearby towns or distant cities, in the days when North Carolina was just one big neighborhood—were occasions of great pleasure to her. (Martha Emily Moye Hadley 543)

Few are privileged to enjoy the host of friends that are hers. This is an earned privilege that comes from dedication in serving the community and the capacity for working in harmony. (Miss Virginia Belle Cooper 237)

Space here does not permit a narration of exceptional cultural opportunities afforded Jesse Rountree Moye by her father. The influence of her personal contacts with renowned figures in the world of the arts is reflected in her varied interests in the community life of Greenville and Pitt County. (Jesse Rountree Moye 543)

Study Guide

Kristine Handley
Period 6 / 10·30·95

- Know vocabulary and people
- Understand sequence of events
- Worksheets
  A. English Exploration
    1. Spanish/English rivalry
      a. How did this affect English settlement?
      b. Why was Amadas/Barlowe voyage important?
      c. Lane colony's problems
      d. Lane colony's purpose
      e. Lessons learned by Lane's attempt.
  B. Lost Colony
    1. Problems
    2. Fate?
- Know importance of Raleigh's voyage

Queen Elizabeth Philip Amadas
Humphrey Gilbert Virginia Dare
Walter Raleigh
Richard Grenville

Her idea of honoring the first child of English parentage born in America, who was Virginia Dare was one of her dreams, which was achieved by Sallie Cotten. She later wrote a booklet poem, *"The White Doe: the Fate of Virginia Dare."* She arranged for the construction of a great desk, to be on exhibit at the fair, carved from holly wood grown on Roanoke Island depicting the legend of the white doe. (Sallie Southall Cotten 240)

A man whose formal education was no more than thirty weeks of "schooling" between 1884 and 1894 [age 7-17], he nonetheless became the epitome of the self-educated person. In the summer of 1895, he took, and passed, the North Carolina State Teaching Examination. For the next twenty years he taught school. (Charles Kelly Dunn, Sr. 277)

NORTH CAROLINA PUBLIC SCHOOLS

Certificate of Honor

This Certifies That

Kristine Langley

of the Sadie Saulter Elementary School,

has made the honor roll for the entire school year 19 92 19 93 and is now entitled

to this certificate of distinction.

Given this 9th day of June 1993

Pitt County

Administrative Unit

Mrs. Robyn Newfor
Teacher

Reba R. Dailey
Principal

He became principal of the C.M. Eppes High School upon the death of the principal, Mr. Charles M. Eppes. Later Davenport became the Supervising Principal of the three Negro schools here, Fleming Street School [Sadie Saulter], South Greenville School [Wahl-Coates], and C.M. Eppes High School. (Willis Haynie Davenport 267)

NORTH CAROLINA PUBLIC SCHOOLS

Certificate of Honor

This Certifies That

Kristine Langley

of the C. M. Eppes Middle School,

has made the honor roll for the entire school year of 19 94 -19 95 and is now

entitled to this certificate of distinction.

Given this 2 day of June 1995

Pitt County Schools

Administrative Unit

Gen Adams
Carolyn Terebee
Teacher

Principal

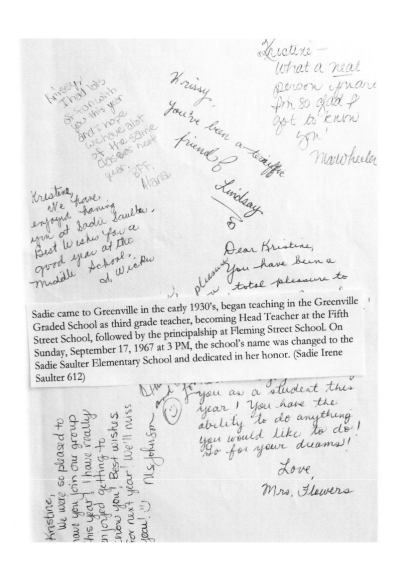

Krissy!
I had lots
of fun with
you this year
and I hope
we have alot
of the same
classes next
year.
BFF,
Mara

Krissy,
you've been a terrific
friend.☺
Lindsay
☺

Kristine—
What a neat
person you are
I'm so glad I
got to know
you!
MaryWheeler

Kristine,
We have
enjoyed having
you at Sadie Saulter.
Best Wishes for a
good year at the
Middle School.
J. Wicker

Dear Kristine,
please You have been a
total pleasure to

Sadie came to Greenville in the early 1930's, began teaching in the Greenville
Graded School as third grade teacher, becoming Head Teacher at the Fifth
Street School, followed by the principalship at Fleming Street School. On
Sunday, September 17, 1967 at 3 PM, the school's name was changed to the
Sadie Saulter Elementary School and dedicated in her honor. (Sadie Irene
Saulter 612)

you as a student this
year! You have the
ability to do anything
you would like to do!
Go for your dreams!
Love,
Mrs. Flowers

Kristine,
We were so pleased to
have you join our group
this year. I have really
enjoyed getting to
know you! Best wishes
for next year! We'll miss
you! ☺
Ms. Johnson

She also learned that her granddaddy, Leon S. Hardee, once attended school in the first Pitt County courthouse and remembered the bloodstains on the floor. (Goldis Starling Reel 596)

In 1864 Federal troops invaded North Carolina. A group of their cavalry raided the Marlboro area and came upon May-Lew. The Lewis men were off fighting for North Carolina and the Confederacy. The women came out onto the porch and asked them to leave. One of the "Northern Gentlemen" ungraciously fired his weapon at her. He missed but the shot went into the back chimney on the east side of the house making a hole big enough to put a child's fist in. It remains to this day as mute testimony of the ungentlemanly character of some Yankees (and their bad marksmanship!) (Benjamin May Lewis and Artimissia Baker 455)

On rainy days in the 1890's, their grandson would play with the worthless Confederate money which was kept in an old trunk. This grandson also recalled that former slaves of his grandparents, who had adopted the family name as their last name, would frequently make visits to his boyhood home at Rives' Landing in order to keep in close touch with the family members. (The Rives Family of Rives' Landing 599)

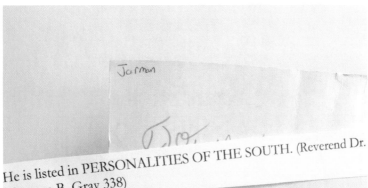

Downeast North Carolina Regional
SPELLING BEE
Sponsored by:

DAILY NEWS and PCS Phosphate

Kristine Langley 29

Mrs. Spilman, with the blessing of her husband, ran for office in the North Carolina Senate in 1932, the first woman ever to do so. "I did not win in votes counted," she said, "but I did win in that I showed the state that a woman could make a good showing, yet I had the privilege of continuing to stay at home with my husband and children." (Mrs. J.B. Spilman 636)

C&1-9

Student's Name	Kristine Langley	ACADEMIC PROGRESS REPORT	Date 3-19-96
Class	Grade Eppes	Pitt County Schools	Teacher Ross
Subject L. Skills		1717 WEST FIFTH STREET • PHONE 830-4200 GREENVILLE, N.C. 27834	

INSTRUCTIONS

1. The purpose of this report is to inform you of the student's present status in this subject:
   + (VERY GOOD)   ✓ (SATISFACTORY)   — (NEEDS IMPROVEMENT)
2. A very good performance is to be commended. If improvement is needed, please study the recommendation(s) checked(✓) below as well as additional comments, if any. ITEMS NOT NOTED WERE NOT EVALUATED AT THIS TIME.

CURRENT STATUS:

ABILITY	ATTITUDE	PERFORMANCE
APTITUDE IN SUBJECT	ATTENDANCE/LATENESS	TEST SCORES
FOUNDATION IN SUBJECT	PREPARATION FOR CLASS	HOMEWORK/NOTES
MOTIVATION	APPROACH TO STUDIES	ATTENTION
WORKING TO POTENTIAL	RESPONSIBILITY	PARTICIPATION/COOPERATION

Proud of standing in the spelling Bee

RECOMMENDATION(S):

CONTINUED GOOD PROGRESS	STUDY THIS SUBJECT EARLY IN THE EVENING	IMPROVED PREPARATION
IMPROVED EFFORT	IMPROVED CLASSWORK	AFTER SCHOOL HELP
PARENT-TEACHER CONFERENCE	MORE SERIOUS APPROACH TO STUDIES	TUTORING

ADDITIONAL COMMENTS: *Poetry Notebook - 93*
Test - 97
Quizzes - 100, 100, 100
Unit Test on poetry - March 29

PARENT SIGNATURE:

PARENT'S COPY-WHITE   OFFICE COPY-PINK   TEACHER'S COPY-YELLOW

William got a B.S. degree from E.C.U. in Business, and his wife a B.S. degree in Medical Records Administration from E.C.U. He is associated with his father and brothers and she is Tupperware Manager. (The Peter Brown Family 202)

Beautiful hats with willow plumes or egrets, flowered chapeaux and panne velvet toques are stored with her mother's Brussels lace gown, now yellow with age—a black pointe de sprit, sprinkled with sequins and with jet beaded yoke, a black velvet cape—nostalgic reminders of halcyon days never to return. (Novella Higgs Moye Williams 540)

No picture ever did justice to her lovely countenance of patrician features, flawless complexion, violet eyes, and long brown hair, not a strand of which turned gray to the end of her life [at age 87]. (Novella Higgs Moye 538)

With her passing has gone one of the last vestiges of an age and a way of living almost forgotten. In her latter years it seemed that she was trying to recapture some of the happiness of former years, the unhurried and nostalgic days when, as the gentle mistress of her Southern plantation home, she kept her heirloom silver gleaming, floors waxed, fine china ready for afternoon tea, the summer houses abloom with roses, and her horse and carriage ready to accommodate a chance visitor. Miss Mary was born in Reconstruction time—March 29, 1867. (Mary Louise Mewborn Worthington 760)

Also buried with the family she loved is the faithful friend who refused to leave after she was granted her freedom when the South lost the war. She was affectionately called "Aunt Mahalia," and is loved even today by family members who never saw her, but know her story well. (George Murray Watson 703)

In the summer of 1978 Mrs. Olive Lang Shearin and I visited the abandoned home of Olive's grandfather, my great-grandfather Gideon Ward, located in Pitt County on Little Contentnea Creek, about six miles west of Farmville. The structure remains straight and sound, but is superficially in bad repair, the two-story front porch fallen down, the clapboard cover paintless and weathered, the windows boarded up. It is a large house. Entering the front door, which faces an extensive grove of oaks to the east, one enters a central hallway on the right side of which is a stairway leading to the second floor. The first door to the right enters the master bedroom in which is a second stairway, to the bedroom above. Olive pointed out that, to enter or leave their own bedroom, the daughters had to pass through their parents' bedroom. The door opposite the master bedroom reveals the front parlor with its beautiful wainscoting, but missing mantle. Past the stairway, doors lead to more rooms before the door at the back end of the hall opens onto the back porch, which gives access to kitchen and pantry. Upstairs are, in addition to the daughters' room, partitioned off from the rest, three bedrooms along the hall, all to the left, and separate quarters, accessible only by third stairway, over the kitchen. There are five chimneys, providing each room with his own fireplace. The old pot straps hang intact in the large kitchen fireplace. (Gideon Ward Family 699/700)

There is no one rocking on the porch any more and no one tending the garden. (Luther and Clara J. Dail 257)

They are buried on a farm they owned called the Langley place. (Henry Benjamin and Nellie Ayers Harris Family 365)

Aren't all of us proud that we are linked to Pitt County. (The Eubank-Bryan-Whitehurst Families 296)

Aren't all of us proud that we are linked to Pitt county?

Assessing

What do I do with a county that puts its jail bookings on the front page of its online newspaper, the *Daily Reflector*, displaying photos, names, charges? What do I do with a county that routinely arrests citizens for reasons such as "COMMUNICATING THREATS" and once, inexplicably, "HABITUAL FELON"—the only crime that a man was once a felon, nothing else in the indictment? It's been over twenty years since I lived there and I know my classmates have grown up. I don't expect to recognize anyone by their face alone. But I have always been good with remembering names, so I click through page after page, looking for the misbehavior of someone I knew.

There is a newer section in the *Daily Reflector*—it's appeared in the last two or three years—called "Bless Your Heart," a thinly veiled column of shit-talk, anonymously collected through emails sent to blessyourheart@reflector.com, where Pitt County residents can complain about their neighbors, the government, the collision between more than one point of view. A recent example: "So, remove the Confederate monument from the Pitt County Courthouse grounds to the Confederate graves section in Cherry Hill Cemetery, unless you are so offended by those Confederate dead that you also want them removed, BYH." It's a Letters to the Editor gone wild—no one has to sign a name to their opinion, no one has to face repercussions for calling another out. It's all drawled with that fake concern I remember from middle school—*does she really think that she belongs here; bless her heart*—double-speak, double meaning.

The *Chronicles of Pitt County* is a flawed record of history, but what does it mean that I have leached its facts into my mind, trusted the tellers, pieced together family histories based on information from the year I was born—before the internet, before Ancestry.com, before my classmates began the Facebook mistake of oversharing on nonprivate accounts?

Pitt County was the place where I learned doublespeak, but it is also the place where I took generosity for granted. There were kindnesses done to me that go unmentioned, easily forgotten by my need to polarize and accuse others of causing what I did not internalize. I had teachers who watched out for me—both locals and transplants—scooping me up from the travails of messy friendship dissolutions and putting me somewhere safe, the back of a classroom where I could work on a project, alone. I also had friends who did not turn on me—girls that I harmed out of fear—and yet I easily wave a hand over their kindnesses, reducing them to an anecdotal existence in a neighborhood essay. I could not receive their love without shame that it came too easily, certain that they would have been kind to anyone; I was sure there was nothing lovable about me.

History is a series of filtered facts. But what about all the truth that is ignored, all the lies that codify into veracity simply due to their inclusion in the right places? If I slip my facts into a slit in the seam of Pitt County, will they remain, or like a splinter, will they eventually work their way to the surface and be popped out with a fingernail, a minor invader extracted from the corpus? What if the body itself is rotting from within, a molding peach pit split open at the core, presenting a perfectly healthy exterior?

I participated in the Third Downeast North Carolina Regional Spelling Bee in 1996, the subsidiary bee a girl had to win to get her trip to the big dance in D.C. I had defeated my whole middle school. The announcer at the Downeast Spelling Bee was a local news anchor from Greenville or Kinston. When he gave me the drawled word "poliobolitis," I spelled "poliobolitis." It was wrong, of course, because the word was actually "poliomyelitis," but I couldn't understand the announcer's accent, even after four years of living on the coastal plains. A couple of months later, I watched another girl on television win the national bee with "vivisepulture," the act of being buried alive, what I thought was the story of my life in Pitt County. Honestly, I knew at my core that I wouldn't have known how to spell "poliomyelitis" even if the announcer had spoken more clearly. I hadn't studied hard enough; I hadn't encountered the word before.

But I lied for years as I retold the story of my close call to others, "poliobolitis" floating out of reach, a word I swore that would have let me kick down the bricks of my tomb if I had just understood what was said.

Alignment

I have begun collecting gemstones and leaving them in melamine bowls on my deck when the astrological signs are changing, or when the moon is full, or when rain is expected so I can cleanse them. I read about that practice on a website after I'd googled "meaning of carnelian." I am casting my astrological houses, and I check my Co–Star app in the morning as regularly as I used to read my syndicated horoscope in the Living section of the newspaper. That was back when I invented my own horoscopes out of song lyrics; I wrote down the lines I wanted to guide me through the school halls, and I would draw one of the scraps out of a cardboard box I kept on my dresser top.

Now I wear raw opal and ruby rings during my entire sun sign's reign, and I watch for numerology. I am only beginning this essay because today is 8/1 and eight is my lucky number. It is not only 8/1; it is 8/1/2019 and 2019 minus 8 is 2011, the year Annie died. There is 1 left behind. I look for order because it soothes me; I follow rituals because they are born of experience. I am a cradle-raised Catholic and a cradle-raised liberal progressive, still accepting the closed circuit of a two-thousand-year-old religion because I love the recitation and repetition of ancient prayers. They return me to the girl I was.

I am not supposed to say this, but I prefer the Old Testament to the New because I take comfort in the idea of dictates that no person could feasibly follow—the impossibility negates my failures. I am not supposed to say this, but I stand behind the ambo and read to the people in the pews once a month because I get to interpret God's word, craftily emphasizing my diction to embed my personal understanding into the record. I am not supposed to say this because ecclesiastically, I know better, but the saints are like household gods. I tuck a prayer card for St. Kateri, the patron saint of people in exile, on the fridge; I place her statue on my bookshelf, her unlit novena candle on my desk. I call to Kateri now, though Lucy is my confirmation saint—the girl whose name I took when I was confirmed. I do not ask for Lucy much anymore. I found out I needed glasses when I was seventeen, and since I thought Lucy was the patron saint of eyesight, I figured it couldn't hurt to get her special intercessions. But Lucy is actually the patron saint of blindness, and I have worn glasses for the last twenty years, so.

My parish priest recently told us about the church built atop Golgotha, the site of Jesus's crucifixion. He prefaced his homily by saying, "Now, this is a religious story, not an archaeological story." He said the altar is built directly over the place where the cross was positioned, and after Mass, pilgrims can reach their hands underneath to touch the rock of Golgotha with their bare hands. Dug into the earth one floor beneath that rock, there is a chapel built to honor Adam, because Jesus's death site was aligned over the actual site of Adam's burial. The priest's homily was about ancestral ties, the bonds that elongate and stretch from our rib-creation past into the infinite future. The priest said that when Jesus bled, his blood seeped through the soil to fall onto Adam's skull, which is to say to fall on all of us, since we are all linear descendants of the first human. I imagine how long those bones waited to be redeemed, shifting millimeter by millimeter to position themselves underneath a site pregnant with meaning, a receptacle for the future.

|

I am trying to bring everything into alignment. If I can redirect the bisecting lines of the past and the truth, I can stop them from cutting my heart in half. I was driving to pick up my daughters from camp, listening to America's "You Can Do Magic" on SiriusXM Yacht Rock Radio, thinking about how I generate things into existence. I pulled up behind a car with the license plate letters "ECU," which was the university in North Carolina where my father taught when I was in middle school. The place where Annie cracked my adolescence in two, leaving behind a raw wound that can never heal because the dead cannot accept forgiveness. I can find meaning anywhere. I will find meaning anywhere. I don't think I have given up on the corporeal world as much as I am making another place in case I need it. I do not fault deathbed conversion cases for suddenly trying to rectify all the years they chose not to live by a punitive code—I understand the need to have their bases covered. Didn't God arrange the stars in the sky? Didn't God give us the curiosity and knowledge to find the meanings He imbued in this world? This is how I can hold all of these beliefs simultaneously. I am hooking connecting strings around the forensic evidence on the walls of my conscience.

|

I looked at my daughter's sixth-grade schedule because I wanted to help her learn her locker combination. Her locker number will be 1168, which did not surprise me as much as it hollowed my solar plexus. 1-1-6-8 were the last four digits of Annie's phone number. I had been talking to my friends earlier that same day about how middle school changed me from susceptible to secretive. I was thinking about Annie. I was also thinking about Indiana, our birthplace, the residence we had in common beyond our middle school exile to North Carolina. Indiana was also the place where I refused to know her again in high school once we had both moved back and she tried to return to me. Indiana is also the place where she was buried.

It was 8/1, one month beyond Annie's death date on 7/1/2011. I know it looks like I am grabbing at meaning and I do not care. 8/1/2019: one month later, eight years later, the last four digits of her phone number resurfacing as my daughter prepared for middle school. Annie has spoken through the illusion veil before. Really, I just want to believe she is still speaking to me. I am still listening.

|

I have performed many years of magical thinking, which is

why Joan Didion's book scared me so badly. Didion is famously rational, impassionate, removed, and yet she fell apart looking for order when she lost someone. It is a harbinger I keep on my bookshelf, a reference guide for loss and a checklist to ensure I can find my way back out.

I have so much fear over how unbothered my tightened circle of trust has been since Annie. None of my parents or siblings or daughters have died precipitously; no one has had catastrophe. Something is imminent. It must be. It is not enough to ward the nightmare off with charms and stones. I have to prepare. So I run through scenarios, ones far from worst case, to give myself little tests before the final. What will I do if. What will I do when.

What have I done but arranged the bones just so, devising a tableau of possible mistakes, horrible spells I am afraid I may have called into being?

|

I am fixated on how it looks like I have three planets in my Twelfth House, the house which *The Only Astrology Book You'll Ever Need* calls "the House of Secrets, Sorrows, and Self-Undoing." I cannot believe that eighteen years ago, I encountered this exact same book on a shelf in a dorm room outside of Glacier National Park and now I am studying it, at thirty-seven, like it can give me the explanations I crave. That was more than half my lifetime ago.

Back then, I was obsessed with finding meaning in the song lyrics my ex-boyfriend had quoted in his emails. I was calibrating my own, responding with just enough to tease the tip of what I meant; the rest was there if he searched for it. He did not, or at least he did not let on if he did.

Now I am reading about my Cancer sun and Aquarian moon, tilting my birth time one hour forward to accommodate the daylight savings time that Indiana, actually, did not participate in during July 1982. I am trying to make my computer-calculated horoscope agree that I am a Scorpio rising rather than a Libra. I have no idea if the Cafe Astrology website already knows to do that—I had to google "Indiana time zone" because I remember the state's position changing and shifting, one season in eastern before switching to central, the TV schedules getting all confused. All I know is that every description of a secretive Scorpio rising makes more sense, in my past, than the personable Libra.

It is exhausting making sense of myself.

I think it matters that I am a Cancer sun, pulling people and emotions toward me, and I am also an Aquarian moon, pushing everyone and everything away, declaring the uselessness of emotionality. That is how I choose to interpret my astrological signs. It feels good to think that I am born to push and pull; it takes the burden off my actions.

I explain to myself to keep it straight, paraphrasing from my book: the moon sign is your inner core, the sun sign your life story, the rising sign the way you are perceived by others. I am, at my core, an unemotional person who requires rationality and distance. But my life arcs around the search for home—the mooncrab heart of my hidey-hole—and the desire to scuttle to safety, clutching everything I need. I appear secretive and abrasive and dogmatic, because I am. I am a water sign—a Cancer—and my moon sign is Aquarius, the Water Bearer. I inwardly cling with my claws like a crab, and I outwardly whip anyone who approaches me with my hard-shelled tail—obviously a Scorpio. It all makes sense, but I want it to make sense.

There's more. So much more than I can outline, though I am carefully underlining passages in my *Planets in Houses* and *Astrology for Lovers* books, both undermining my recognition that there is not one Only Astrology Book I'll Ever Need. But I'm trying. There are twelve houses in which the planets can be located, but a person does not necessarily have a planet in each house, or in many. Aquarius's ruling planet is Uranus, which is located in my First House, the house of self-identity. I hold the moon's location in my Fourth House, the house of home. My Cancer sun's ruling planet is the moon; Cancer is the traditional ruler of the home. I am a collapsing Ouroboros, eating my moon in my house and spilling it into the guts of my house, which is built of moon.

In my horoscope, the Twelfth House is granted the three planets of boldness, abundance, and death and rebirth—a Plutonian underworld marked by my dark Scorpio rising. My three-planet stellium, my strongest pull, my Twelfth House—what does it mean to be magnetized by the grief of secrets I have hidden because I cannot undo them?

|

I took my daughters onto a side trail at a nearby forest and the crickets were so loud we couldn't hear much else. We were halfway into the woods, we hadn't encountered another person, and my daughters had paused and turned around to face me. A summer doe suddenly burst from the trees, bisecting our path. She couldn't have been more than eight feet away from my oldest daughter. I was the only one looking forward; it was like the doe ran by just for me. It was the sort of thing a mom lies about to get her kids to shush, *shhhh if we're quiet enough maybe we'll see wildlife.* But I really saw it. The doe was as tall as I was, so large she would have mowed my daughter over. She could have mowed me over. But she did not.

When I was hiking in Utah with my sister, we went off trail behind the Dark Angel in Arches National Park. We were trying our best to follow animal paths to avoid straying onto the biocrust. We were so far away from the main trail that no one else was in sight. We were looking for a specific petroglyph panel and we couldn't find it. Instead, I found a feather right in the middle of the track we were tracing back out. I picked the feather up and tucked the little gift into my hatband, feeling chosen.

It was like the time I was driving my daughters home along a well-driven street near our house in Nebraska. We crossed over a train trestle, and for some reason, I looked down at the tracks. There was a pair of foxes sitting right on the rails, like an omen just for me. My daughters got angry I didn't tell them to look in time, but they couldn't have seen the foxes anyway.

I saw a deer down by the train tracks that run behind my neighborhood a week or so before I left on my trip to Utah. I was in training, walking in the summer humidity with my dog every night so I could manage the impending thick heat of July in the desert. The doe crossed the street just as I happened to cross the same street, looking to see if any cars were coming. My dog did not see the doe, but I did.

They were the same tracks where I believed the mountain lion lived, must have been four or five years ago now. She really did creep around the tracks—there were sightings marked in a mile-wide radius that spring. I watched for the mountain lion every night I drove home from Hy-Vee in the dusk, but I did not see her. Still, it gave me comfort, oddly, to think of the mountain lion at large padding around my neighborhood, circling us in, enveloping suburbia with a presence older than humans. My sister and brother-in-law believe in Animal Medicine. They have cards they draw like tarot, and they watch for animals as directional signposts. Mountain Lion, when I look it up, refers to convictions, and pulling Mountain Lion is a sign that you might be found at fault for the insecurities of others.

The mountain lion was spotted in the wild for several weeks until she showed up at a nearby center for abused children, leaning against the warm cement block right outside an office window. Parks and Game was called, but they deferred to the safety of the children. So the police, instead, aimed their rifles at her and shot six rounds, five more coups de grâce to ensure the mountain lion would not attack. Once she was assuredly dead, Animal Control removed her body, only then discovering the mountain lion's broken leg.

|

I say prayers of protection; I always have. I perform a ritual progression before I can fall asleep, a closing of safe circles, chanting, "Please don't let anything scary be, happen, or do anything in my room, my closet, the rest of my house, around my house, all our property, and everything that affects me." I say an upside-down pyramid of prayers, five Hail Marys, four Our Fathers, three Hail Marys, two Our Fathers, and I close with one final Hail Mary to the woman I trust to guard me. The Bible says help will be given to those who ask, so I ask. Or maybe that was Dumbledore in *Harry Potter*. It doesn't matter; I believe in them both.

|

The full moon in Aquarius approached for the first and only time all year.

I was going to end this essay describing how I gathered my amethyst and calcite, rose quartz and malachite, carnelian and citrine, laid down on my deck in the moonlight and positioned the stones in a rainbow down my chakras. I wanted the planets fixed around me, Mars in Libra in my Twelfth House, bold and fair and weighing the pros and cons of listening for a connection.

But the Aquarian full moon happened on the Assumption of the Blessed Virgin Mary—a holy day of obligation observing Mary's full-body ascension to heaven. So I went to Mass and listened to another lector read from the Book of Revelation. She said, "A great sign appeared in the sky, a woman clothed with the sun with the moon under her feet and on her head a crown of twelve stars." I heard the lector emphasize the word "moon."

The full moon was also Open House Night at my daughter's middle school. She showed me how she could open her locker—start on 47, spin to 29, go back two notches to 27. Annie was 29 when she died; I met her 27 years ago. Will I still be circling around the sorrows of my life when I am 47? Will I still be performing semiotics on what it meant when my younger daughters arrived home that same night and told me they had slowed down at the train tracks because my middle daughter could sense there was a fox—*and there was*—and they all saw it, but I didn't?

Everything is already in alignment. But I am looking for it. I know.

Pull Me Through
the Doorway

It was a town as hard to penetrate as the pine windbreaks planted in the pocosins around the tobacco fields, dense fences even during the off-season when the curing shacks were abandoned and the cracks in the boards widened and no one fixed the hinge on the door and it was left open, just a sliver, an invitation or a warning: something lay inside. Would I be brave enough, or stupid enough, to approach?

I spent hours under the overhang of my front porch in North Carolina, watching the neighborhood from a spot where I could see but not be seen. I see myself on that porch all the time, a mnemonic for my self-positioning and how I believed someone would look deeper to find that girl selecting into her loneliness by refusing to come into the light.

So many of my memories, upon reexamination, have revealed more of my own blame than I expected. I wrote and then erased the entire story of Captain from the narrative of my friendship with Annie. Captain was a girl who sat at our lunch table in middle school and also took horseback riding lessons at the same stables Annie frequented. Annie and I called her the Captain because she was brisk and efficient, taking notes in her daily planner, spastically rubbing her nose with her pointer fingers. Captain would settle herself down at our lunch table and remove a Thermos of milk and a note from her mom, written on cutesy, holiday-specific stationery from *Current* magazine, reminding Captain to take her Lactaid. We lambasted both Captain and her mom for single-handedly ruining the environment by wasting paper. At first, Captain tried to stand up for herself, but two against one meant we always won.

When we learned about the Iron Curtain in social studies class, Annie and I came to lunch armed with a plot. Annie had diagrammed a note with blueprints for alienation. We arranged my clarinet case, my lunch box, Annie's violin case, and Annie's lunch box in convex angles, taking up as much table space as possible. Captain protested, asking us to put our stuff on the floor, but we retorted, "It's the Iron Curtain. You can't move the Iron Curtain."

A couple of months later, Captain brought us red heart-shaped Christmas ornaments from FAO Schwarz, wrapped with bows and hand-lettered name tags addressed "To my Lunch Buddies." Annie and I freaked out—did the Captain think we were *friends* with her or something? I worried that Captain would start calling us to play with her after school, so Annie decided we should shave Captain's horse. I didn't know why, but I didn't argue. Annie just wanted to shave Captain's horse. We were going to shave her horse if we could have just found out where she lived. We were going to show up, razors in hand, and we knew Captain would be so scared she'd run and hide behind the stable, petrified. She wouldn't be able to stop us, wouldn't even be able to move. We thought we were that powerful.

The cruelties of those years are stored like evidence boxes in a back room, labeled with pseudonyms and shorthand so I could forget precisely who was who, and who really did what. I swear that the reasons used to be clear and obvious, but now the pain of being hurt is all that remains, though I don't know whether it is my own pain or the pain I inflicted. I am waiting for someone to pull apart my chronicles and reveal what I still refuse to see.

It is a place I will never leave, a girl I will never leave, a splinter my skin absorbed that my body refuses to reject. I can see that splinter, black like the megalodon teeth I picked out of the creek banks, exposed after millions of years only for an interloper like me to pocket and take them away. What did it mean to live somewhere so old that dinosaur sharks had left rows of teeth, shedding one jaw width only to grow another? What did it mean to live somewhere so young that the teeth were still there after all those years, after the local kids had taken what they wanted?

I smuggled my ancient shark teeth in the bottom of cardboard boxes and moved them to the next house, the next state, where I lost them, the teeth slipping between the four-by-eight joists of my attic. I think about the archaeologists who will sift through the decay someday, when the insulation has degraded and the house has been pulled apart and the wreckage has been shoveled into the town dump. I can see, glistening in an excavated midden, those misplaced teeth giving everyone the wrong impression. Megalodons never moved over the ancient Midwest. The sharks lived in North Carolina, behemoths silently gliding through the water, mouths closed to hide the threat.

They had claimed the South would rise again, but I wanted to see it rise from God's own wrath when a hurricane swamped Pitt County three years after I left. I was glad to see the destruction on national television, glad to watch the milky-brown river rage twenty feet over flood levels, sliding across the flat landscape of the town where I felt like I was left to drown. I wanted to see my old house half-underwater, but my neighborhood was too far away from the river; there was just a handful of downed trees, the same aftermath as every storm.

It was a town that poured out sweet tea for company after I'd angrily stomped off the porch; a town quietly pouring a fresh foundation as I'd kicked at the rotten exterior; a town that brought me to my knees with that old adolescent desire to belong, willing to take the hazing if it meant my forearms would be clutched, pulling me through the doorway into the darkness, leaving the others outside.

Acknowledgments

Thanks to Derek Krissoff, Sarah Munroe, Sara Georgi, and Than Saffel for the love WVU Press has put into publishing my book. Thanks to Elena Passarello and Jeremy B. Jones for selecting *Curing Season* to be a part of the In Place series—a dream home for this book that dreamed of being firmly rooted in place.

Thanks to Jeremy and Erica—your reader reports made me burst into tears because you saw *Curing Season* for what it is. I still have your words taped above my desk as encouragement. Being seen is the greatest gift an author can receive, and I am so grateful.

Thanks to all of my writing teachers, particularly Pam Gasway, who saw an extremely early version of "Not Something That's Gone" and told me I was writing nonfiction—a comment that changed my entire life's trajectory. Thanks to Marilyn Abildskov, whose early support at Iowa was a turning point.

Thanks to the English department at the University of Nebraska–Omaha. I am indebted to Yvette and Doug at the

Kinney Family Foundation for the John J. McKenna Graduate Fellowship, and the University of Nebraska system for the Presidential Graduate Fellowship, both of which permitted me to focus my full attention on developing as a writer. Jody Keisner, John T. Price, and Lisa Knopp—how can I thank you enough? I brought you a chorus line of experiments for three years and you gracefully welcomed my tests on the boundaries of nonfiction while offering considered and critical feedback. Your questions, suggestions, dedication, and advocacy have been incalculably valuable.

Thanks to the editors and readers at the journals where versions of these essays originally appeared: *Blood Orange Review*, *CHEAP POP*, *DIAGRAM*, *Little Fiction/Big Truths*, *New Delta Review*, *Pithead Chapel*, *Quarter After Eight*, *The Rumpus*, *Speculative Nonfiction*, and *Sundog Lit*. Thank you for pulling my essays out of the piles and giving them space.

Thank you, additionally, to Robert Atwan for naming "Alignment" a Notable Essay in *Best American Essays 2021*.

Thanks to all the readers who were generous enough to offer feedback during the development of these pieces, particularly my fellow writers in the Barrelhouse workshops and at UNO.

Thanks to my online writing friends, especially my Split/Lip Press family. Thanks to my offline friends who embrace my ALL CAPS emails and texts because you know I love to yell when telling a story.

Thanks especially to:

The girls-by-a-different-name in *Curing Season*, particularly Heidi and Emily. Thank you for accepting my flawed adolescent friendship; thank you for accepting my friend requests years after we knew each other. There are layers of truth and I'm only scratching at the surface.

Shannon Carter, Lily Glenn, and Grace Van Berkel—the Ladeez who believed I would write a book and laughed with me through those golden MySpace blog and Evading Mwomdom days.

Lauren Bonk, Erin Casey, and Sarah Duncan—my SLEK sisters for nearly ten years (!), your daily love, righteous indignation, and astrological insights delight me. I have your group note, written the day I found out this book was accepted, taped above my desk too. See you on the Polos!

Emily Howard, since the first day of freshman biology and forever after, the plans I make still have you in them. My backup memory since 1996, my best friend, the only person besides my parents to buy all the print journals where I've been published—thank you for being you.

My wonderful and supportive family, especially my siblings, Kate and Eric, and my parents, Dave and Trina: the holy host of others standing around me. You are the bedrock that stabilized all my transplantations. I love you immensely.

My daughters, the delights of my life, my curious pioneers, my wild tornadoes, my mischievous charmers wandering through early adolescence and all its breaks and bends: Kirsten, Annike, Britta, this book is for you.

Kevin, always my first reader, who has spent twenty years watching me sleepwalk through my past and still patiently waits for me to reach out a hand: you pull me through the doorway every day and every night.

And finally, my thanks to Pitt County, North Carolina: the real place and the reconstruction. No matter where I lived, my adolescence would always have been packing season, leaving season, replacing season, curing season. Sometimes, when the light slants just right, I think I see you.

In memory of E.A.Y.

Notes

Epigraph

The epigraph is kindly borrowed from page 148 in Linda Flowers's sociological history *Throwed Away: Failures of Progress in Eastern North Carolina* (University of Tennessee Press, 1990).

Shadowbox

For more information on the Leverian Collection/the Holophusicon and Sir Ashton Lever, I recommend Adrienne L. Kaeppler's *Holophusicon: The Leverian Museum* (Museum Fur Volkerkunde, 2011) or, for those of you who prefer your history truncated, "How Sir Ashton Lever Curated the World—Then Lost It All," by Allison McNearney for the *Daily Beast*, November 23, 2018 (https://www.thedailybeast.com /how-sir-ashton-lever-curated-the-worldthen-lost-it-all).

A Fixed Plot

If you weren't fortunate enough to remember your eighth-grade North Carolina history textbook, more details on the Lord Proprietors can be found in the *Encyclopedia of North Carolina*, edited by William S. Powell (University of North Carolina Press,

2006). Google Maps provided significant intel, as did WikiTrees, the website Cemetery Space (www.cemetery-space.org), and Facebook. The interview with the Pitt County resident can be found at "New Homes Confront Old Burial Grounds" by Kate Galbraith for the *New York Times*, June 17, 2007 (https://www.nytimes.com/2007/06/17/business/yourmoney/17natreal.html). The City-Data forum for coastal North Carolina referenced in this essay can be found at https://www.city-data.com/forum/coastal-north-carolina/860833-graves-peoples-front-yards-2.html. April M's quote is taken from "A Hidden Cemetery at the Mall" by Liz Mays on Eat Move Make, September 18, 2012 (https://eatmovemake.com/concrete-covered-cemetery-mall-parking-lot/). NC State Code GS 65–106, Part 4 delineates the legalities of moving graves in North Carolina. The helpfulness of Bill Kittrell's contributions to the Cemetery Census archives (cemeterycensus.com/nc/pitt/about.htm) cannot be overstated.

Not Something That's Gone
Quoted material from Margaret Atwood's novel *Cat's Eye* (Doubleday, 1989) appears within this essay in bold and italics.

Out Line
Chronicles of Pitt County by the Pitt County Historical Society Inc. (Hunter Publishing Company, 1982) is referenced. For more on C.M. Eppes Middle/High School, see "C.M. Eppes Legacy Lives in Two Schools," *Daily Reflector*, February 27, 2011 (https://www.reflector.com/news/local/c-m-eppes-legacy-lives-in-two-schools/article_5b6fba72-c07a-5de5-819b-831e9c14239b.html). To read about the history of desegregation in Pitt County

Schools, see the "Unitary Status" page on the Pitt County Schools website (https://www.pitt.k12.nc.us/domain/47).

A Pit Is Removed, a Hollow Remains

Excavation Report refers to *Chronicles of Pitt County* by the Pitt County Historical Society Inc. (Hunter Publishing Company, 1982). For more on the false history of Henry Lawson Wyatt, see "N.C. Revises Its Civil War Death Rolls Downward" by Martha Waggoner for the Associated Press in the *Free Lance-Star*, June 13, 2011 (https://fredericksburg.com/local/n-c-revises-its-civil -war-death-rolls-downward/article_ccd3074e-5f5f-520c-b456 -ea7b26f6d365.html).

Grafting's family history quotations are taken directly from the *Chronicles of Pitt County*, and grafting quotations are adapted from *The Grafter's Handbook* by R.J. Garner, revised and updated edition (Chelsea Green Publishing, 2013).

Piecing and **Replacing** have quotations taken directly from the *Chronicles of Pitt County*.